RIDING

THE BALANCED SEAT

Riding

BY
BENJAMIN LEWIS

INTRODUCTION BY
COLONEL JOHN K. BROWN

PHOTOGRAPHY BY
EUGENE FRIDUSS

De Luxe Edition

THE GARDEN CITY PUBLISHING CO., INC.
GARDEN CITY, NEW YORK

TO A PATIENT WIFE

PREFACE

We have attempted to put into permanent, practical form a modern system of basic riding instruction that will result in a firm, balanced seat on the horse—a seat that will at the same time give the rider control of the horse, riding comfort and style—whether he prefers the bridle path, the hunt or show ring.

"Riding" is a regular course of basic instruction to be given the reader in person. The successive steps of training have been carefully chosen only after thorough analysis and test. Insofar as practical the book was prepared in the order in which it is presented. It is the result of several years' observation, study and testing on both beginners and experienced riders.

The main conclusion drawn from our experience is that the art of riding a horse may be taught best by example.

Next most important is that few riders have a comprehensive idea as to what a good seat should be and how to go about acquiring it.

The third is that "seat" has as many descriptions and forms as there are instructors. This despite the fact that all horses are similarly constructed.

Another is that the rider, in order to acquire the benefits of one system of training should do all his learning on one well-mannered, well-trained horse until the rider's confidence and basic training are both definitely and firmly established. The horse must also be able to assist the rider, if only to withstand the effects of beginner's handling.

Still another is that in the average school too much emphasis is placed on putting the rider in motion before the rider correctly understands what, where, when and how.

Experienced riders and beginners with whom we have discussed training problems have long expressed a need and desire for a basic system so arranged and in such simple form that in it both rider and instructor find mutual understanding. Such a book, too, should take the "mystery" out of learning to ride properly within a reasonable time.

The reader may feel, at this point, that like so many other books on the subject, this one, too, will attempt to "talk down" to the beginner from the heights of life-long experience. Far from it. A moment's study will show him that the entire design of this book is from exactly his eye-level.

These are some of the reasons for our doing a book using action photographs exclusively. We have tried to make the pictures just as permanently interesting, self-explanatory and instructive as time and photography would permit. We have kept strictly to the rider's viewpoint, both physically and mentally, by showing rather than telling. And therefore, we use one rider who may well be the reader himself, learning to ride one horse thoroughly, by one basic system.

THE RIDER

The rider we selected is Mr. Robert P. Stout, from whom we have received most constructive cooperation. An experienced rider himself, he agreed that the riding world needed such a work. But the question of his ability to act the part honestly caused him to hesitate.

Before a single picture was made for this book, conferences were held between Mr. Stout and the author. Experimental photos had already been made in which the author himself did the riding. Based on analysis of these and the author's previous research, Mr. Stout and the author spent many very interesting hours discussing the various phases of basic riding instruction.

One day, we had an opportunity to show the application of our system on two untrained riders, who were having difficulty getting their horses to do as they wished. The author, using these two strangers, took the opportunity to show them and Mr. Stout the difference between even the slightest proper basic training and none at all. A few minutes' demonstration showed that even those horses would respond to the aids when properly applied.

Mr. Stout decided that the experiment of being a student for the period of the book would be most interesting to try—if not a positive aid in his study of equitation method. He threw himself whole-heartedly into the job. In order that we might better show the reader what a rider's back actually looked like during training, he also agreed to ride without a tailored riding coat. We ask you to study the pictures carefully as to consistency of purpose.

Although originally it was our intention to use a beginner or an untrained rider as a model, the time element made the idea impractical. And we feel now that, with Mr. Stout's efforts, we have been even more successful.

The few pictures in the book showing wrong form were not especially made. They really occurred as we tried to get the pictures needed. The

photographs have even enabled the rider to correct his few heretofore un-
noticed faults, and naturally they will do as much for you.

THE HORSE

We chose a horse neither of us had seen before. We had our selection of
several offered by kind people interested in our purpose. We chose Cadet
because his type, training and temperament were equal to that of any good
school horse, although he happens to be privately owned. He has been
trained to the usual aids and to jump up to 2½ feet, which is as high as
necessary for basic training. His personality, too, impressed us as being
highly desirable in a beginner's horse.

Yet Cadet is not the "perfect" horse. He has the same whims and ob-
stinacies (usually called ideas) any horse might have. While this book is not
intended in any way to encourage you to attempt to train a horse, it so
happens that the regularity of our system did have a definite effect on
Cadet, in that his past training was enhanced by continued proper use of
aids, seat and handling. We did not attempt to reach the limit of his schooling, but rather to have him do well the few basic movements our course
covers.

Take Cadet as your own. You'll enjoy the ride. His step is cushioned, his
mouth is soft, he enjoys doing as you wish, if you will only learn to ask him
quietly, and above all, clearly.

THE OBJECTIVE—A BALANCED SEAT

What is a "balanced" seat and why? Is it the popular so-called "forward"
seat derived from the Italian school?

Our system has been worked out only after thorough testing. It has a
definite objective as to seat, general horsemanship, and comfort for the rider.
Knowing how successfully many of our friends have ridden the balanced
seat for years, we feel that you will come to the same conclusion as to the
system's sensible method and advantages.

The balanced seat was introduced and developed in this country by Lt.
Col. J. K. Brown, Cav. U.S.A. As chief of the equitation department of the
U. S. Cavalry School at Fort Riley, he instituted what, in effect, is this system. As you now see it, it includes the results of the author's study and experimentation. Col. Brown has been kind enough to write the Introduction
to "Riding" in which he discusses the seat and other modern riding ideas.

However, to visualize immediately what is meant turn, for a moment, to page 57 for a comparison with the following description.

A balanced seat is that position of a mounted rider when he sits balanced on the horse, in the lowest part of the saddle, leaving a space of at least a hand's breadth between his breeches back and the cantle. The body is easily erect, balanced on a base consisting of seat, thighs, knees and stirrups; chest high and just forward of the true vertical. The back is hollow, waist relaxed, head erect, shoulders square.

The seat and legs are close to the horse without pressure, knees down and closed against the saddle in front of the stirrup straps. Thighs, knees and calves turned in to the horse. Lower legs are brought back under the seat and rest lightly against the horse; stirrup straps vertical, feet at least halfway home in the stirrups, ankles bent, heels down to the limit, toes out slightly. With the eyes directed downward the rider will not see his toes.

All strength in the balanced seat is by sheer weight, not grip—during normal movement at the slower gaits.

All movement is forward from the rider's seat, through the horse's shoulders.

The horse moving forward, his center of balance precedes the movement. Your control of balance is in your weight above your seat. Therefore, your point of balance will be moved forward (from the waist up) proportionately with that of the horse. See pages 106–107.

The arms are extended to make a straight line to the horse's mouth through the wrists and through the reins when the horse's head and neck are extended. The elbows bend slightly just forward of the body, but hang from shoulders naturally. Hands, thumbs on top, are closed lightly on the reins feeling the horse's mouth by flexing of the fingers and separated evenly across the horse's withers.

This *does* balance you literally on your seat, in exactly the right spot on the horse's back, just to the rear of the withers. Your center of gravity is directly over the center of gravity in the horse. You therefore represent the least possible load to the horse and should feel yourself "part of the horse."

You will find that having acquired this seat, a minimum use of aids will be necessary to get immediate and correct response from the horse at any gait.

The balanced seat, assisted by the flexibility of the waist and back, and the "clinging of the thighs to the saddle," gives you a secure position which is not easily dislodged even by unexpected movements of the horse.

THE "FORWARD SEAT"

At the shows today you see a majority of "forward seat" saddles. Yet the riders generally ride their usual seat with the thighs almost horizontal, lower legs straight down, weight far to the rear and reins too long. As soon as the horse, in approaching the jump, picks up speed, the rider's toes reach down and the back is hunched over while the hands push on the horse's neck. That is not a true "forward seat" though many people mistakenly think it is.

The Italian forward seat as used by experts, usually military riders at the big shows, is the extreme form of our balanced seat.

The school of *basic* equitation in Italy calls for a balanced seat as we have already described—even though in such details as length of stirrup, placement of hands, etc., they may differ slightly from this book.

In general, the faster you travel, the further forward and out of the saddle goes your seat. The stirrups are shortened to suit your personal needs. Instead of on your buttocks, which now you extend to the rear almost on a rising plane, you balance on thighs, knees, stirrups and *motion* of the horse. The reins also must be shortened. This extreme form of the balanced seat should be used only by advanced students and then only for short periods of fast show jumping or across country. Under no other conditions can you ride comfortably and safely, perched on a horse's shoulders.

In this book we do not show any examples of the extreme forward seat. Our Cadet neither travels fast enough, nor were our jumps difficult enough to require anything but normal cooperation on the rider's part. This was accomplished by riding a seat constantly in balance with, and in control of the speed of the horse.

We promise you that if you do enjoy our system of training, and learn to ride a balanced seat, you will be well on your way to the correct form of the popular forward seat, and with a competent instructor, go on to success at the hunt or in the show ring, from where we leave you—soundly trained in the simple basics of modern riding technique.

In conclusion, we wish to add that this book *is* addressed as sincerely to those interested in saddle classes. We repeat, the principles of the balanced seat do not change, because the horse does not—all the hybrid riding styles of today's show ring to the contrary, notwithstanding.

Your own experimentation will prove that the balanced seat is the most graceful seat, even for the show ring. A study of current *dressage* photographs from the Olympics will prove that the balanced seat is here for good.

ACKNOWLEDGEMENT

The author wishes to thank his many kind friends for the generous encouragement and assistance rendered, without which this work might not have been possible.

MR. EUGENE FRIDUSS
for his unfailing genius with the camera

MAJ. GEN. FRANK R. McCOY, U.S.A.
Commanding General, 2nd Corps Area
and
COL. ALBERT S. WILLIAMS, 16th Inf. U.S.A.
and staff for permission to use Governors Island and its facilities

COL. GEORGE M. RUSSELL, Cav. U.S.A.
Chief of Staff, 61st Cavalry Division and staff

LT. COL. JOHN K. BROWN, Cav. U.S.A.
for his training, technical advice and Introduction to "Riding"

MAJ. CATESBY apC. JONES, Cav. U.S.A.
for the use of his horse, "Cadet"

MAJ. ROBERT P. STOUT
303rd Cavalry
for his many invaluable services

and to the many civilian friends who have listened patiently all these years.

BENJAMIN LEWIS

INTRODUCTION

Equitation is a very difficult subject to teach and consequently good riding instructors are comparatively rare. General L'Hotte, one of the greatest of French horsemen, has expressed the difficulty thus: "In order to instruct in equitation, even the elements, one must know a great deal. . . . In order to understand instruction in equitation, the student must be able to *feel* the instructions."

Equitation is based upon mechanical principles and common sense, both of which are as old as the hills. As all riders and all horses vary, and neither are mechanical, controlling a horse so as to get the most out of him for any desired result, is truly a great art. To become an artist in any line requires good instruction and a great deal of time for practice and experience.

It is an unfortunate truth that most Americans think they can ride, whether they have ever had any instruction or not. It is also unfortunate that many people think they can instruct as soon as they have learned a very few things about riding. This accounts, in part, for the horrible examples that are often seen on the bridle paths and in the country. Another factor in poor riding is the element of conceit. Many people resent being told that they are doing anything incorrectly. Others ask for criticism of their riding for the sole purpose of being told how good they are. This fact has caused many experts to withhold any advice, even when asked for it.

As in most forms of athletics, anyone can learn to ride the right way quicker and with less effort than he can the wrong way. Having learned to ride the wrong way, it may be harder for one to correct his bad habits than it was to learn riding in the beginning. Therefore, to begin with, it is of the greatest importance to select the best system of basic riding instruction.

Modern thought considers any system of athletics wrong which does not include rhythm and balance. This is especially necessary in riding a horse—where the rider's every movement and position must be in rhythm with the horse's movements in order to maintain security and not interfere with the capabilities of the horse. As the horse that is poorly balanced may pull, stumble and pound so much that he soon becomes unsound with use, so will the poorly balanced rider who is not co-ordinated with his mount cause the horse to do all of these things and many others. In addition, unless he is able to remain relaxed, the rider will work one muscle against another in attempting to maintain security, which makes hard work of a sport. This in turn greatly reduces the benefits and pleasure which anyone should obtain from his riding.

But, if a system of equitation instruction is so important, how can one find out which is the best system? Hundreds of books have been published, yet about the only similarity in some of them is that the rider is advised to sit astride a saddle on the horse's back and control him with the reins. In most modern countries the style of riding has changed greatly since Tod Sloan introduced the "American Seat" to racing in Europe about thirty years ago; and changes have been even greater in the past fifteen years.

It seems reasonable that one should inquire of those who are up-to-date on the theory of equitation—today's best and most successful riders. Or, would *you* ask someone who was a good rider fifteen to twenty years ago and who has not learned anything new in equitation since that time?

Some twenty years ago I heard a major who was about the worst rider in my regiment, say that it would be a waste of time for him to go to Fort Riley, (the U.S. Cavalry School) because having ridden for thirty-five years, he could not learn anything there. He, of course, did not realize that there are no perfect horsemen. In contrast, we read that James Fillis, who was one of the world's greatest riders and horse trainers, stated that after fifty years of teaching and experimentation he learned one of the most important principles of equitation. This should cause us, at least, to keep our minds open and be ready to accept new ideas of proven worth.

At the Cavalry School in 1922, when I began changing the then accepted seat to the "balanced" or "forward" seat, I met with considerable enthusiasm on the part of the younger officers and a great deal of opposition from some of the seniors. This was as it should be. The Army has ever been slow to change its methods and thus has generally avoided the rule of faddists. I remember an amusing conversation with one colonel who would not admit that there was anything good about the forward seat. He remarked that he could ride a horse only once or twice before his mount would begin to buck after every jump. Yet it was quite evident to anybody who watched him ride that he leaned backward during the last half of the jump, bumping the horse's loins sufficiently upon landing to cause resentment. Believing that his seat was perfect, however, he could not be persuaded to change.

I took hundreds of photographs at Fort Riley to prove that the correct way to jump a horse is for the rider to lean forward, with his buttocks off the saddle while approaching the jump, during the entire jump, and until the horse takes a stride or two after the landing. The rider thus avoids certain negative reactions and assists the horse that much. With the "balanced seat" there is no good reason for doing otherwise, except a clinging to tradition.

Also by photographs, I proved that the best way to ride down a very steep slope or slide is to take about the same position as when descending from the jump; i.e., the body bent forward from the hips, nearly parallel to the horse's neck, back straight, head up, buttocks just off the saddle and thrust well to the rear, the buttocks and hips acting as a counterbalance for the upper part of the body, no change in position of the legs, the reins very short for control, with hands low beside the horse's neck. This may sound difficult, but if you have any strength in your legs, you will find it comparatively comfortable and an easy position to assume. Its adoption almost eliminated strained jockey muscles, of which there had been a great many among the students. It is much easier for the horse also, because he has freedom in using the muscles of his back, loins and hindquarters.

For purposes of instruction at the Cavalry School, I caused a soldier to be trained as a movie photographer. It took him so long to gain the necessary experience, however, that he was not of much value until after I left the School. Had I had an accomplished photographer to help me, such as Eugene Friduss who took the photographs in "Riding," my task would have been greatly simplified and the results more lasting.

My early knowledge of the forward seat was gained entirely from analysis of the seats of successful or outstanding horsemen, and my own experiments. I knew nothing about the Italian method until I had used the forward seat for several years for polo, horse shows, and cross-country. When I did have an opportunity to learn something of this method, I was glad to find that my own conclusions were very similar to the Italians'! The Italians' claim that they were the first to use the forward seat is probably correct, but any statement to the effect that everyone who has used the forward seat has imitated the Italians, is incorrect. No doubt others have had experiences similar to my own.

When I was at the French Cavalry School at Saumur, I found that the seat I had already adopted was about the same as that in use by the French, except that my position was somewhat further forward and my legs carried a little farther back so as to make the stirrup strap vertical. I learned much about the use of the hands from the French, and through riding their well-trained high school horses, I gained a thorough knowledge of the use of the aids, which I could not have obtained in any other way.

Though I had used the balanced, or forward seat for several years, I was not convinced that it was the right thing for all kinds of riding until I had given it a thorough trial in hunting the difficult country about Pau, in the southwest of France, with its great "talus." Then I knew that with slight modification it was suitable for racing, polo, steeplechasing, cross-country, hunting, as well as for saddle horses, dressage and high school riding.

Through his own ingenuity and perseverance, Benjamin Lewis presents here a system of basic instruction of which I have not seen the equal. As a Reserve Cavalry Officer he has been a star member of my riding class in the 61st Cavalry Division for three years, so our ideas are in perfect accord. He has, through study and hard work, developed the power of analysis without which no riding instructor can be very efficient. In logical sequence he has depicted the intimate details of learning to ride in such a way that anyone should be able to understand them. It is a knowledge of these details and their careful and habitual practice that really makes good horsemen. Carelessness and neglect of details characterize the poor rider. While this book is essentially for beginners, many a rider who has spent years in the saddle can improve his riding by a careful study of the pictures.

While there are various ways of mounting, you can easily demonstrate to yourself that for a beginner with a trained horse, the method shown in "Riding" is the easiest—because the rider mounts immediately to a balanced position over the horse without any twisting. This allows him to settle gently into the saddle without bumping down on the horse's back. The method shown of settling into the saddle is most important and should never be neglected. If you require your horse to stand still while being mounted and never to move until you are ready for any eventuality, you may save yourself a lot of grief, and it also helps discipline the horse. Obedient horses and dogs, as well as children, make the best citizens and are most useful in any community.

In "Riding," among the things worthy of note in the photographs taken from overhead, is the fact that the horse actually does bend from head to tail while making a turn when the aids are correctly applied. A study of these pictures and a little experimentation should convince anyone that it is much better not to use a pound of pull on the reins when an ounce will do the trick.

The system of equitation shown herein differs very little from that used by the United States Army and taught at the Cavalry School at Fort Riley, Kansas, and at every regimental or post riding school for men, women and children throughout the United States. This system is not due to any one man's work, but is the result of the study, experimentation, travel, and endless labor of many intelligent Army officers over a period of years. Together with the experience gained at home, they have combined the best from the European schools to give us a good American seat for American people. The fact that all Army officers are not good riders is nothing against the system. It is not possible for everybody to become an expert rider, no matter which system is followed. The average person has a better chance of learning well with the balanced seat than any other method that has been produced to date.

When a better method is found it will surely be adopted by the Army. War is the most up-to-date thing in the world, and there is very little in the arts and sciences which it does not employ. In spite of all the advances made in motors, nothing has yet been found which can take the place of well-trained horse cavalry. If war were to break out tomorrow, any army commander who did not have a large force of horse cavalry to maneuver at his command would be greatly handicapped. In order to be of value at the decisive moment, cavalry must be able to march great distances rapidly and still be able to maneuver and fight. This can be accomplished only if the horses are well handled and properly ridden. Therefore, it behooves cavalry officers to be skilled in a riding method which requires the least effort from mount and man. This has been found to be the system of the balanced seat.

I want to recommend this seat particularly to owners of saddle horses, as they have generally been the slowest to adopt it. Some saddle horses already are being very successfully shown using the balanced seat. As this seat has been found to be suitable for *dressage* and such high school movements as the *passage* and the *piaffé*, where great brilliance and height of action are required, why is it not suitable for riding saddle horses, either three or five gaited? For many years I have watched good saddle horses in the show ring, stepping high in front but dragging their hocks behind, because the rider sat on the cantle of the saddle and crushed the horse's loins to such an extent that any brilliance of action was impossible. With the weight off his loins, the horse can more easily engage his haunches, and the helpful use of the balanced seat would soon eliminate, in part, the great amount of force which we often see exerted on the horse's mouth in order to collect him. Force, in general, does not cause lightness.

The following passage which I translate from James Fillis "Principes de Dressage et d'Equitation" (Paris 1890) is apropos:

"The fundamental principle that stands out from the studies that I submit to the public, is that it is necessary to search for balance, lightness of the horse in forward movement, in impulsion, in order to obtain the most energetic results by the least effort.

"Balance by the height of the neck flexed at the poll, not at the withers;

impulsion by the hocks engaged under the center; lightness through the re-laxation of the jaw; there you have my equitation in toto.

"When we know that, we know everything and we know nothing. We know everything because we find these principles in all things. We know nothing because there still remains putting them into practice."

I want to recommend a study of this balanced seat particularly to those ladies and gentlemen who are called upon to judge equitation or "good hands" classes in the horse shows. It is very evident at times, from the results, that the judges have not taken the trouble to investigate the "forward seat," "perched seat," "balanced seat," or whatever it may be called. The majority of the good young riders today use the balanced seat, or something very close to it. From close association, I know that some of them change to what I have recently heard called "the toe and kidney seat" when they know that the judge favors the old fashioned saddle horse seat. The "good hands" classes in horse shows which have been encouraged by the American Society for the Prevention of Cruelty to Animals have had a most beneficial effect upon young American riders, but the judge who is not as modern as the exhibitors is certainly a block to progress.

There should be no difference in the seat on a hunter, polo pony or saddle horse except, perhaps, the length of stirrup. The mechanics, the balance, and the rhythm are the same in each case. Eventually this fact will be realized by all.

Benjamin Lewis has used good judgment in calling this the balanced seat, as "balanced" is most descriptive of what the seat really is. I do not favor the term "forward seat" because many people think that a rider is using it if he falls over on the horse's neck while jumping, no matter what happens to his legs and balance. The term "perched seat," I think, carries too much the idea of extremely short stirrups and resultant lack of security. The balanced seat should have a medium length stirrup and should afford the greatest possible security.

I believe that Mr. Lewis' work will be a great assistance to many new riders; for others it will clear up any mysteries which they may imagine, and for any-one it should drive home the simplicity and usefulness of the balanced seat.

JOHN K. BROWN,
Lt. Col., Cavalry, U.S.A.

RIDING

THE BALANCED SEAT

LET'S BEGIN—

HERE'S YOUR HORSE

His name is Cadet. Age seven years. Chestnut and sixteen hands high. He's a nice horse.

For future reference, this is the general geography of the horse.

The left side of the horse is called the near side. The right side is the off side. The withers are the highest point above the shoulders where the neck joins the back.

The forehand of the horse is all of him to the front of a vertical line dropped from behind the withers and includes the forelegs.

The hindquarters include the entire rear of the horse beginning in front of his hips and including the hind legs.

The body of the horse, between forehand and hindquarters, is called the barrel.

Remember, all the time, over sixty per cent of the horse's weight is on his forehand. To keep him balanced in the same proportion means, therefore, that your added weight on his back must be as far forward as his construction allows.

It is on the large ribs, just back of the moving shoulders and other moving muscular power, that the horse carries you. This position of your weight, forward, leaves his hindquarters free to supply the motive power.

In the picture above, you see a broad highlight formed by the contour of the back, just behind and below the withers. This contour is formed by the largest ribs of the horse, and in the lower picture to the left you see the same contour on *both* sides of him. Notice too, that the horse's body is narrowest at this region.

The view at the left shows Cadet in a pose almost identical with the larger photo above. He appears uneven on both sides. That is because his feet were not evenly placed as he stood under the camera. The right hind foot is more to the rear. This is important to you at this stage. It is a hint to remember that your horse is not mechanically four-square—he is alive and his body is constantly in motion, like yours.

The bridle we use almost entirely throughout our course is the double rein—snaffle and curb with movable side bars. This outfit gives you a soft but complete control of the horse during your training period. The reins we use are shorter than on the usual bridle by about six inches on each side. We will show in practice later why reins as used by most people are unnecessarily long.

The essential parts of the bridle are the reins, bits, curb chain, head straps and throat latch, or strap.

The reins are attached to the two different iron "bits" you see coming out of the horse's mouth. The top or snaffle rein is attached to the snaffle bit through the big round ring, as you see. The cross bar of this bit as it goes through the horse's mouth is made up of two short, rounded pieces of iron, joined endwise and flexibly. Even when you pull the snaffle rein hard, it is still a mild control.

The lower rein is called the curb and does what its name implies. It is attached to the vertical side bars of another iron bar that runs across through the horse's mouth too, but below the snaffle. This cross bar has a half moon bend in the middle, called the port. The port extends upward in the mouth about half an inch beyond the top edge of the bar itself. The side bars and cross bar make up the curb bit. Study the lever action a pull on the curb rein will give you. This pull, or curb, on the horse is triply effective because the highest point of the side bar is brought forward and downward exerting pressure through the straps on top of the horse's head. At the same time, the curb chain—which is attached to the top ring of the side bar and now hangs loosely behind the chin—is brought up tight against the bone of the lower jaw. The cross bar in the mouth is naturally unyielding except to twist and press the tongue and jaw. These are sufficient reasons for you to learn to use the curb rein sparingly.

The heavy strap running around Cadet's face is called the nose band. It is purely decorative during this course. The throat latch, as you see it, simply keeps the bridle from slipping off the horse's head. It is opened to permit the bridle to be taken off and on. The brow band is below the horse's ears.

When examining the bridle have your instructor or stableman show you what to look for and how to put it on.

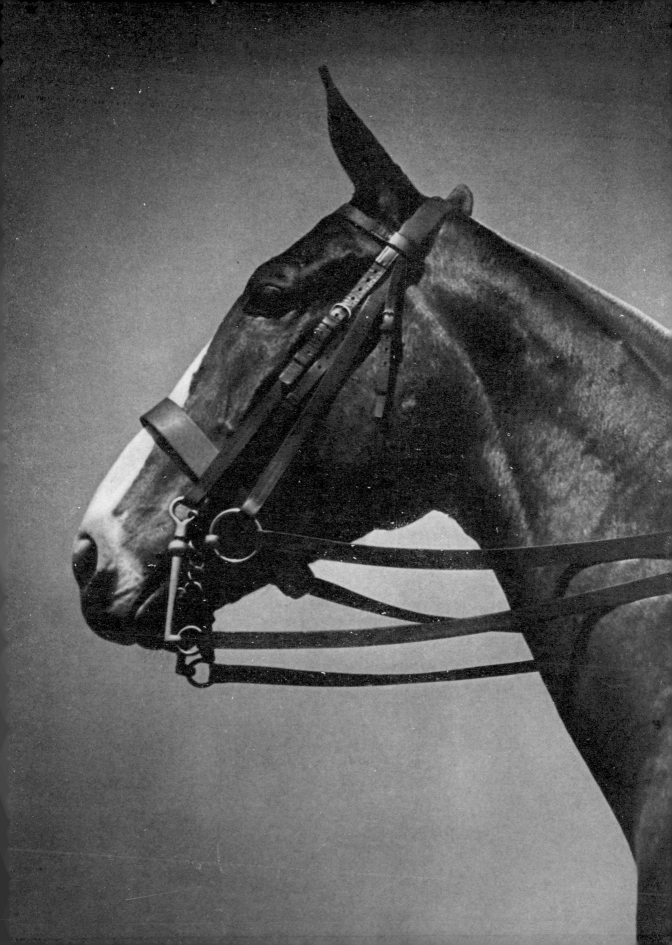

THIS IS THE MODERN ITALIAN-STYLE SADDLE

Only for the student who has mastered the objective of this course, the "balanced seat," is this saddle suitable. Usually ridden with a shortened stirrup, its extremely thick padding at the front edges (knee rolls) helps to serve your legs with a firm base while traveling at high speed over a jumping course. You are not now ready for such a saddle. At the proper time you will be taught its correct use, in detail.

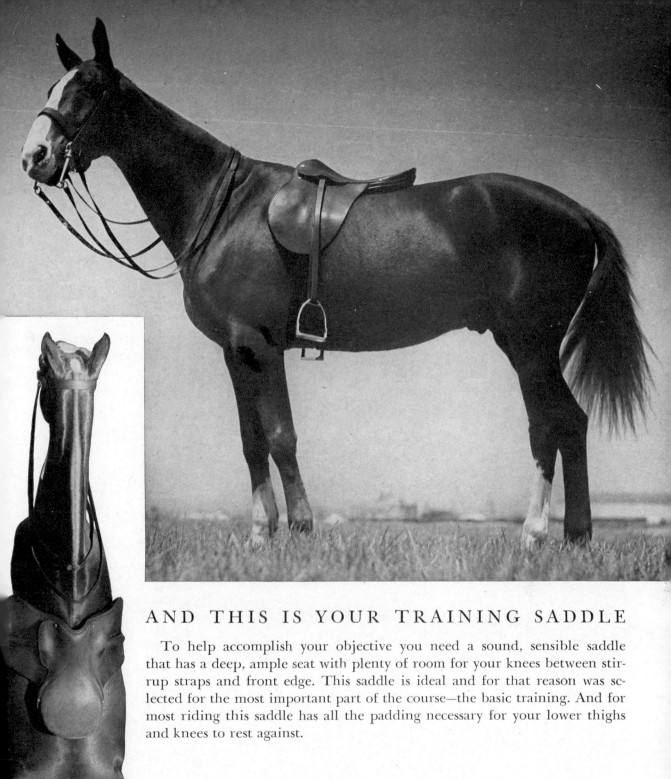

AND THIS IS YOUR TRAINING SADDLE

To help accomplish your objective you need a sound, sensible saddle that has a deep, ample seat with plenty of room for your knees between stirrup straps and front edge. This saddle is ideal and for that reason was selected for the most important part of the course—the basic training. And for most riding this saddle has all the padding necessary for your lower thighs and knees to rest against.

BECOME ACQUAINTED

Practise now, at the very beginning, to be at ease with your horse. Learn now to approach your horse at a walk, always—and if at all possible, from the front. It is advisable to start talking to him quietly as you draw near; and particularly if you have to approach him from behind.

Practise being quiet near your horse. Talk quietly to him and pat him easily, but in definite, smooth, comparatively slow actions. Remember at all times not to make sudden motions in the horse's view. If you do, it will cause him eventually to doubt your good will.

If you are unfamiliar with horses, arrive early enough at the stable to give yourself a few extra minutes to become better acquainted with your horse.

You cannot learn to ride if you are nervous or excited. Your feelings are relayed to the horse instantly and your ride is spoiled.

When the horse feels in your calmness the confidence he must have, he will be ready to cooperate in helping you to learn to ride.

Now, approach your horse—quietly, from the near side if you can, so that your right arm will be raised even with his mouth.

1. Placing right forefinger between the two snaffle reins about six inches behind chin, close hand, but not tight. Stroke him gently on neck with left hand.

LOWER LEFT

2. Now relax right hand and slide it up snaffle rein on near side. Place left hand through the rein. This leaves the snaffle rein over your left arm when you remove right hand.

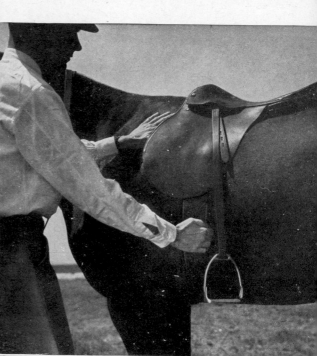

UPPER RIGHT

3. Rest your left hand firmly on the horse's shoulder. Try to put the fingers of the right hand between the girth and the horse. Pull on the girth in order to do so.

4. If more than the first half of your fingers can go behind the girth, tighten it by adjusting straps you will find under the skirt. Test again with fingers. Try not to pull girth too tight.

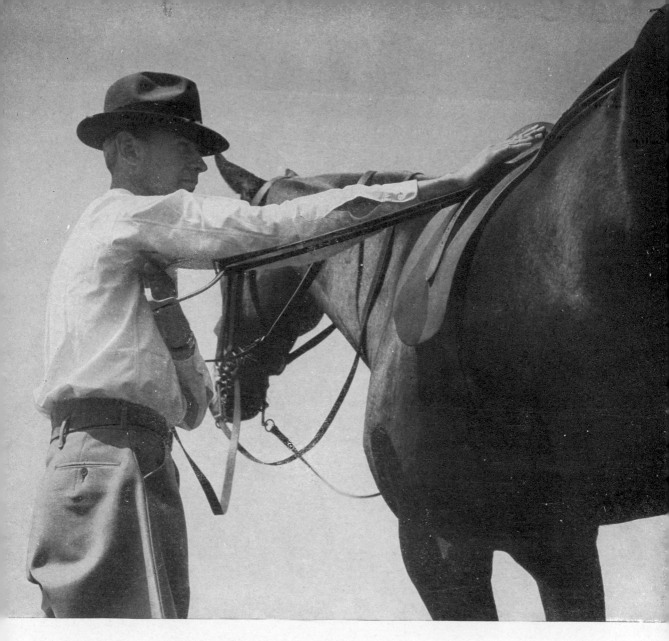

With the snaffle rein loosely around your left elbow, step back alongside the horse and face the saddle. Pick up the stirrup iron in the left hand and place it against the body as you see. Step away and see if length of strap permits your right hand to reach out and rest the fingertips on the near side of the pommel at the seam. If necessary, adjust the strap at the buckle underneath the flap. Make a mental note of the strap hole number for future use. While going around the front of the horse to adjust the other side, drop left, and slip your right arm through the right snaffle rein.

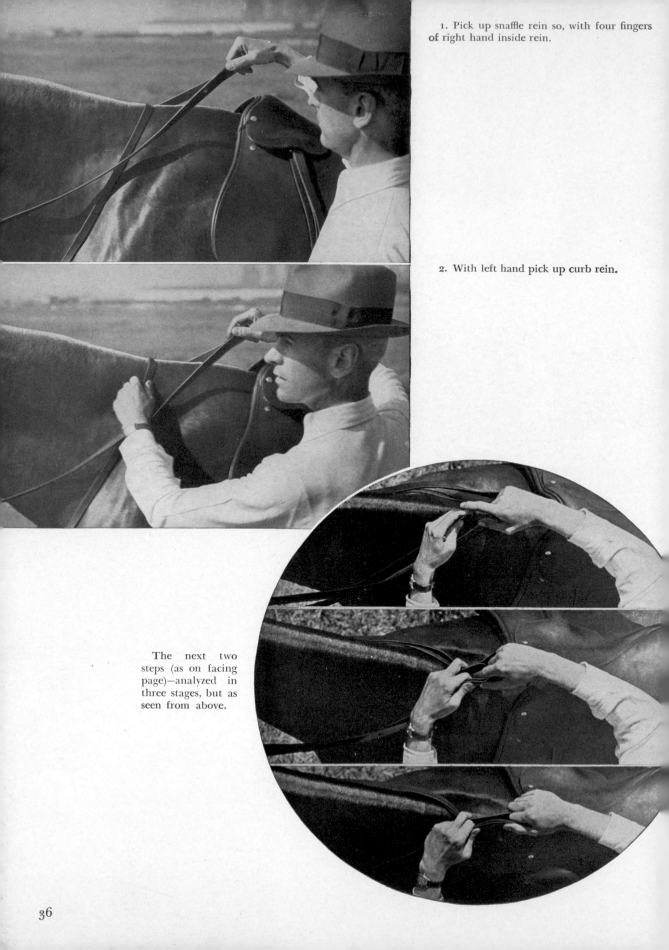

1. Pick up snaffle rein so, with four fingers of right hand inside rein.

2. With left hand pick up curb rein.

The next two steps (as on facing page)—analyzed in three stages, but as seen from above.

3. Extend forefinger of right hand as your left forefinger presents loop of curb rein.

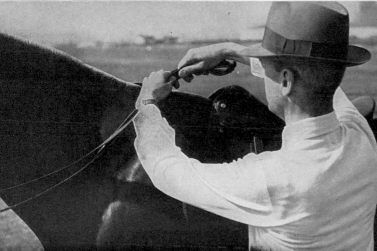

4. Place the right forefinger in middle of curb rein and close fingers on reins. With right forefinger separating both reins, pull reins evenly with right hand through left hand until you feel light contact with horse's mouth.

5. Slide right hand down on reins so that bight (portion of reins not used) forms behind and down.

6. Release left hand and place right hand, which is now in control of horse, firmly on pommel.

You are now ready to mount.

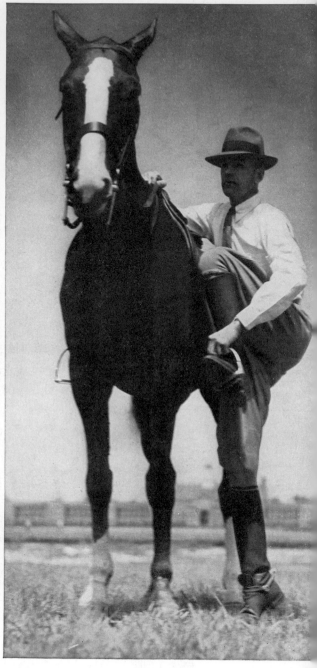

Stand close alongside rear half of the saddle so that your right arm and shoulder are over horse's back. With left hand hold left stirrup in downward grip. Face your body in a line diagonally between horse's shoulders. All movements slow, deliberate.

Raise left knee and foot high. Place foot past the middle, into stirrup and close knee to saddle, tight. Shift weight to your left foot in stirrup. Your body is inclined forward now and still in a line diagonally between the horse's shoulders.

Release left hand and place firmly in front of right, low on horse's neck. Flex your right leg and ankle as you take a deep breath. Spring up, from your right foot, in a line diagonally between the horse's shoulders, keeping your left knee tight against horse. Weight on left foot until you reach the top.

Your weight must be entirely on your hands as you rest, balanced diagonally across the horse's shoulders. Left foot lightly in stirrup, right hanging away. Now, analyze this same position in the next two pictures.

Weight on your hands, balancing your body directly over the horse's shoulders. Only the correctness of this position makes the next movement possible.

NOTE: This system of mounting does two things for you and the horse. It teaches both of you self-discipline in slow, deliberate movements and gives the rider complete control of his balance all during the process. The quiet, balanced weight you place on the horse will (in contrast to other mounting systems where the horse starts off as you leave the ground) encourage the horse to remain in place. He finds out soon enough that you are *not* going to come pounding down on his back. Such is the result of tests using this system on a good many horses with different riders. Compare the other systems with this one right now.

Still using your hands as a fulcrum, take a breath, and swing your right leg in an athletic manner freely and gracefully, high and over the horse's back. Do it slowly—first, last and always.

As your right leg comes down on the far side slow it up gradually, your weight still on hands.

As your right leg comes close to the horse, begin to put some weight into your left knee and heel, bending the ankle. Keep stirrup strap vertical. Let yourself down slowly, evenly, into the saddle. After you sit down place your right foot in stirrup.

Your seat in the saddle should *feel* as you see it now—head and chest high, shoulders back, body erect and relaxed. Seat *down* in the saddle, your thighs, knees and calves directed downward and fitting snugly to the horse, but by *weight*—not grip. Ankles bent, *heels down*, toes out slightly—as the stirrup straps remain vertical. Reins in right hand in front of you, over the horse's withers. Place free hand behind you, flat on the saddle—and its breadth fills the space between breeches and cantle. This helps check the correct position in the saddle.

1. Fingers on left hand spread, place them between reins so that left snaffle will be outside little finger.

2. You see now the left snaffle rein nearest you, then left curb, then right curb and last, right snaffle which comes between middle and forefinger.

3. The right hand holds the bight of the reins and brings it over and forward between forefinger and thumb which is raised to permit it to come through.

4. Left thumb closes down on the bight firmly as the right hand releases it to fall in front and to the right.

The left hand holding reins. Fingers vertical, back of wrist straight but relaxed, thumb closed lightly on reins as they come up through the hand and drop over to right. Hand should feel horse's mouth lightly through reins, which it does by a slight flexing of fingers. The reins in order as you see them, beginning from the bottom, are left snaffle, left curb, right curb, and right snaffle.

EXPERIMENTAL NOTE

The thumb in the picture above is extended beyond the fingers underneath. With many riders, this position of thumb would restrict the muscles at the back of the hand and reduce flexibility of fingers and wrist. Try it, by flexing your hand at the wrist. But now, see if holding the thumb *bent down* (on to the bight) allows the freedom of movement you need.

The right hand is brought over in front of left. The little finger is inserted between right snaffle and right curb. The other fingers come between the two pairs of reins as you see.

Bring away the right hand, as you see, separating the reins.

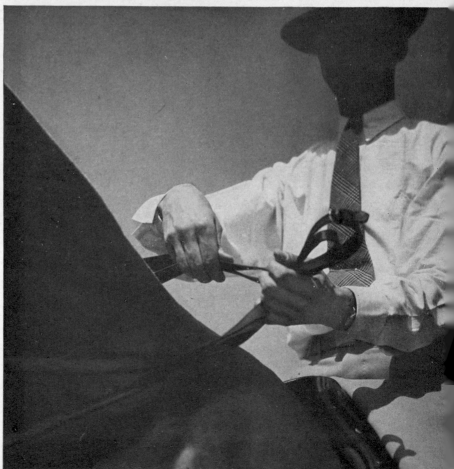

The bight falls to the front and between the reins to the right side of the horse. The fingers are again vertical with thumbs closed on the reins. The snaffle reins come in from outside the little fingers, the curb reins come in between the little and next finger, then up through the hands, and forward between thumbs. Hands separated evenly across horse's withers, about 9 inches apart. The rest of the body has not moved. Study the position in detail.

Weight evenly distributed, hands evenly separated and in contact with horse's mouth. Legs close without pressure, heels down, toes out slightly.

THE SEAT

HOW TO ACHIEVE SECURITY
AND EASE
IN ADDITION TO APPEARANCE

You sit nicely in the saddle, looking secure and sure of yourself. And naturally, you are ready to ride off, but please don't! It is true that your seat in the saddle *feels* secure but could you maintain it with the horse moving? What if Cadet suddenly turned to welcome his stablemate across the field?

Your problem, at this point, is *not* to learn to ride off, but to *stay where you are*, quietly, and *study the mechanics* of your position on the horse.

Remember, first, there is no need for hurry.

Remember, too, that the objective of this course is to teach you how to *acquire and maintain the seat* on the horse correctly in balance with him under any and all circumstances. This takes time and training, but the rewards are worth the effort.

Study the following pages conscientiously. The progress of the movements shown is based on experience and constructive research. Properly and carefully executed, *not* just imitated, they will help you acquire the flexibility that is so necessary in maintaining a secure seat. This flexibility or suppleness is what makes it possible for you to sit comfortably on a live animal, and meanwhile learn to control it.

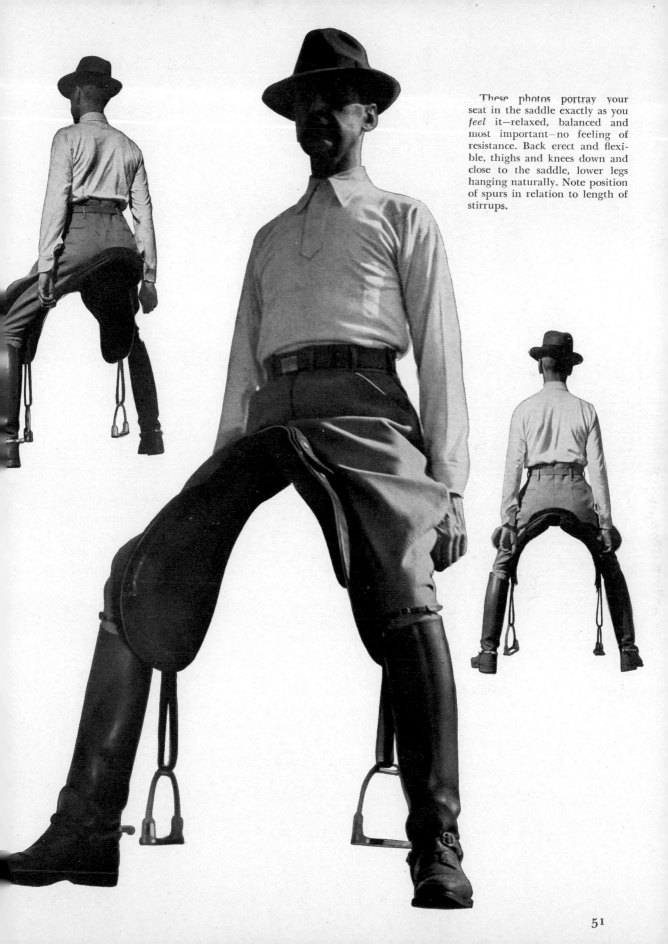

These photos portray your seat in the saddle exactly as you *feel* it—relaxed, balanced and most important—no feeling of resistance. Back erect and flexible, thighs and knees down and close to the saddle, lower legs hanging naturally. Note position of spurs in relation to length of stirrups.

51

This is really the preceding picture, but *on* the horse. Note position of your knees. Note lack of resistance with complete weight in the seat. Practise spreading your legs out and back until you feel the uppermost inner corners of the thighs close to the saddle.

Reach your free hand down in back to the inside seam of breeches. Take a strong hold, pull back and up turning the thighs in so that entire leg to the toe is turned in to the horse. This brings thighs and knees closer to the saddle. Practise with the other hand and leg too, shifting reins, of course.

TO ATTAIN NATURALNESS, CONFIDENCE AND STRENGTH, SEATED ON THE HORSE

These exercises are simple and easy to do but very important. They teach you to relax and develop suppleness in the saddle. Remember to do these and others of your own invention whenever you reach a quiet spot. Do them all deliberately and slowly, with feet out of the stirrups. Ten minutes at least, of every hour should be given over to these exercises.

UPPER LEFT—Lean forward easily from the waist. Reach out and stretch the body to stroke the horse's head. Try to retain hollow, relaxed back.

DIRECTLY BELOW—Swinging your arms alternately, describe vertical circles to the rear. Wrists soft, hands loosely open. Repeat, slowly.

NEXT BELOW—Horizontal suppling exercise. Twist your upper body slowly at the waist, around as far as you can go, and then reverse. Arms relaxed. Palms up. Repeat.

TOP RIGHT PICTURE—Reins in one hand, reach around to the horse's back and pat him there with your free hand. Try it with reins in other hand.

LOWER RIGHT—Lift one knee as high as possible without shifting the seat—lower slowly, and then alternate with other leg. In lowering legs in turn, extend each one to limit, reaching downward. Keep the back straight but relaxed.

OTHER EXERCISES are suppling of the ankle by rotating movements. Try alternately and in unison. Flex hands, wrists and arms in the same manner. Invent ways to increase limberness of neck and shoulders. They're lots of fun and very helpful.

OUR OBJECTIVE

A Balanced Seat is that position of a mounted rider when he sits balanced on the horse, in the lowest part of the saddle, leaving a space of at least a hand's breadth between his breeches back and the cantle. The body is easily erect, balanced on a base consisting of seat, thighs, knees and stirrups; chest high and just forward of the true vertical. The back is hollow, waist relaxed, head erect, shoulders square.

The seat and legs are close to the horse without pressure, knees down and closed against the saddle in front of the stirrup straps. Thighs, knees and calves turned in to the horse. Lower legs are brought back under the seat and rest lightly against the horse; stirrup straps vertical, feet at least halfway home in the stirrups, ankles bent, heels down to the limit, toes out slightly. With the eyes directed downward the rider will not see his toes.

All strength in the Balanced Seat is by sheer weight, not grip, during normal movement at the slower gaits.

All movement is forward from the rider's seat, through the horse's shoulders.

The horse moving forward, his center of balance precedes the movement. Your control of balance is in your weight above your seat. Therefore, your point of balance will be moved forward (from the waist up) proportionately with that of the horse. See pages 106–107.

The elbows bend slightly just forward of the body, but hang from shoulders naturally. The arms are extended to make a straight line to the horse's mouth through the wrists and through the reins when the horse's head and neck are extended. Hands, thumbs on top, are closed lightly on the reins feeling the horse's mouth by flexing of the fingers, and separated evenly across the horse's withers.

This does balance you literally on your seat, in exactly the right spot on the horse's back, just to the rear of the withers. Your center of gravity is directly over the center of gravity in the horse. You therefore represent the least possible load to the horse and should feel yourself "part of the horse."

You will find that having acquired this seat, a minimum use of aids will be necessary to get immediate and correct response from the horse at any gait.

The Balanced Seat, assisted by the flexibility of the waist and back, and the "clinging of the thighs to the saddle" gives you a secure position which is not easily dislodged even by unexpected movements of the horse.

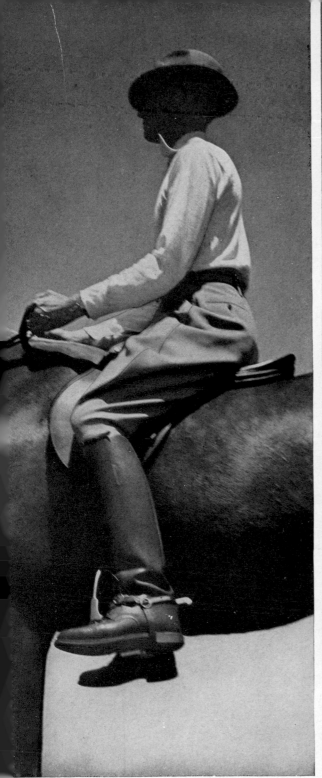

"CHECKING" THE SEAT

Your body relaxed and limber—reins in both hands, chest up but not inflated, thighs and knees se to saddle, legs hanging naturally.

2. Place left foot in stirrup as you see. Do not shift knee. This action should be almost entirely in the lower leg, ankle and foot.

NOTE: *We cannot stress sufficiently the importance of these two pictures and the following three showing how to check up on your seat in the saddle. The future success of your balanced seat, as described in "Our Objective," is vitally affected by your application of the process.*

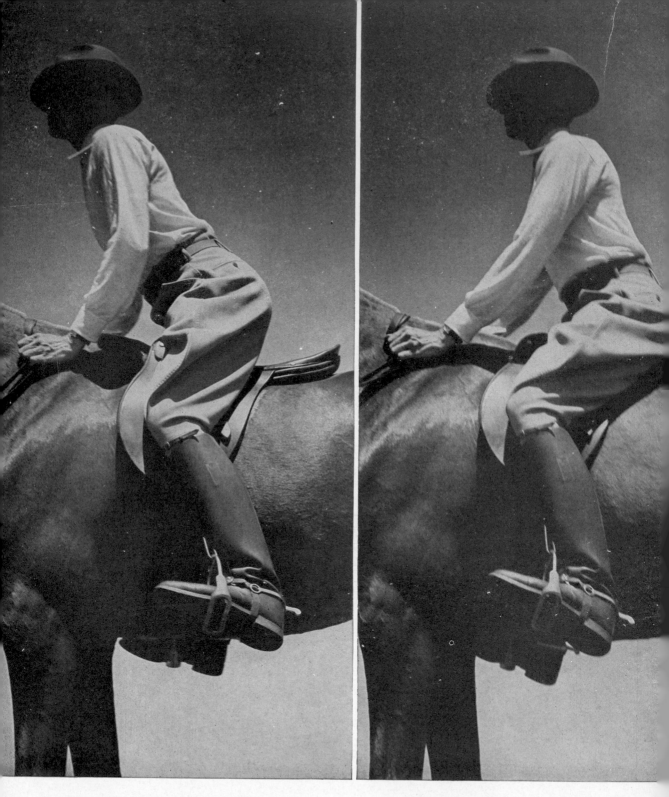

3. Place right foot in stirrup. Hands on horse's withers. Put all your weight on stirrups as you rise in the saddle. Press your heels down, hard!—bending the ankles to the limit—using a spring-like motion based on the stirrups. As you press down, close your thighs and knees in to the saddle by turning in the toes. Extend the buttocks to the rear as you hollow the back to help you push the heels down further.

4. Keep your hands on the horse and sit back and down, slowly. Keep knees and heels in exactly the same position they were when you finished the preceding exercise. Use your knees as a hinge in this action.

You will know at this moment what is meant by the "balanced seat"! Your feeling is that you have made yourself part of the horse. Security and gracefulness is the reward for your effort up to now. Compare your seat mentally with your position when you first mounted. Now—repeat this process of "checking the seat" over and over again. Dismount and start all over again from the very beginning. Learn to see for yourself why you now feel "in balance with the horse."

5. Lift hands away from horse. Knees down and legs under you, chest up, shoulders back, waist relaxed. *This* is the balanced seat! Study it carefully!

LEFT PHOTO:
From front or rear your weight is just as evenly distributed. Compare photo page 50.

RIGHT PHOTO:
Shoulders are square, arms evenly extended, *bent* at the elbows but hanging naturally from shoulders; hands are separated about nine inches, thumbs on top closed on reins. A straight line exists between elbow and horse's mouth when the horse extends his neck and head normally. Legs down and under you. Note saddle showing back of you. Look around and check these things. Hasn't this period of exertion been worth the effort?

DISMOUNTING

Dismounting properly is as important in the self discipline of a rider as mounting properly. The same deliberate care is necessary.

The physical actions are similar to those used in mounting except that the reins require more adjustment, but lightness of action and strength of hands are the same. Dismounting takes only a matter of seconds, and when you study the pictures that follow on the next two pages, in order, you see movie-like simplicity. After rehearsing these steps slowly a few times, you'll do them in a flash, naturally.

To begin, again have the reins in both hands—the first picture on the following page shows first and second finger of left hand "absorbing" the reins. The pictures read vertically, in four columns.

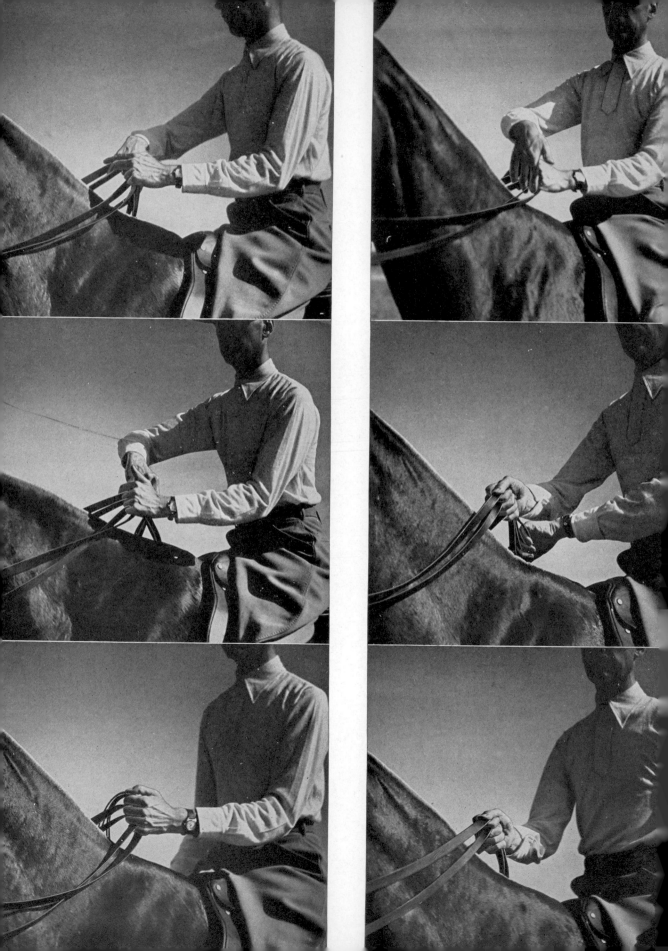

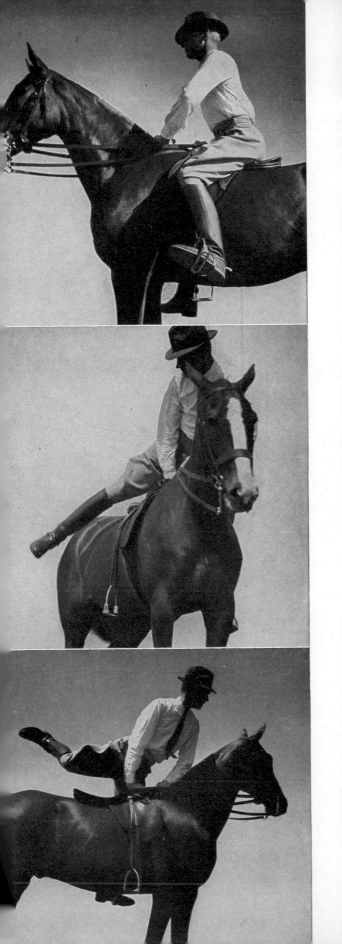

Beginning at the upper left, page facing, the left hand takes reins first, then the right hand, and the bight hangs through the bottom of the fist. The right hand holding the reins is placed firmly on the pommel, the left on the horse's neck, as in mounting. The rest of the process is similar to mounting,—the hands carrying the weight of your body . . . the motions athletic and graceful . . . but when the right heel is brought down on the near side, the left foot is removed from the stirrup and in one graceful motion you spring to the ground at the horse's side, hands on the horse. Then, your right hand sliding down reins, hold him thus.

NOW YOU HAVE LEARNED HOW TO ACQUIRE
AND MAINTAIN A BALANCED SEAT—BUT
WITH THE HORSE STANDING STILL

THE NEXT QUESTION IS HOW
TO START THE HORSE—HOW
TO INCREASE THE GAIT—HOW
TO DECREASE THE GAIT AND
TO TURN AND STOP—IN
OTHER WORDS NOW YOU
MUST LEARN THE MEANS TO
THE END—THE AIDS!

WHICH BRINGS YOU TO THE

PUTTING THE HORSE
IN MOTION
WITH THE AIDS

The aids are Legs, Hands, Reins and Weight of the Rider's Body. Also, when necessary—spurs, crop and the sound of your voice. All these "aid" you literally to control the horse's movements.

The aids are really the only mutual language between horse and rider. There is nothing you can get a horse to do that is not accomplished by means of one aid or a combination of two or more. We will not, at this stage, use any aids but those of the hands and legs. The supposed "genius" you admire in good riders is simply the result of their study in proper application of the aids.

You, too, can acquire that "genius." Having learned to mount to the saddle quietly, checking up your balanced seat by using weight and legs without bothering your horse, you will then be ready to study the application of the aids.

A fidgety rider confuses his horse. It is only logical that the rider who can make his legs and hands move quietly and definitely from one position to another—no matter how slight—will bring about a quicker, more correct response from his horse.

If you will practise sitting quietly, hands apart, with fingers vertical, maintaining the horse's attention forward by slight flexing of the lower fingers only, legs alongside the horse with no pressure, progress is already begun.

Check your seat, using the process beginning on page 55.

When the horse moves forward he extends his head and neck to the front. This brings your hands and body (from the waist) forward to maintain the point of balance. That is why the outlines indicating the body and hand positions vary similarly. These outlines, from right to left beginning at the photo, are the positions at the walk, trot, and canter. The outline to the right of photo is the position at the instant of the halt.

The legs do not act in the above order. They operate in combination with the aids above them only to accelerate or arrest the forward motion of the horse and also to guide his direction.

For simplicity, the positions of the legs are four. No. 1, nearest the horse's shoulder—No. 2 (photo) is next, then No. 3 and last, No. 4, which is no more than six inches' distance from the first position.

Position No. 1—is used generally to hold or push the horse's

shoulder, depending on the desired gait or direction.

Position No. 2—(photo) is the normal position mounted, fe the walk and slow trot. When pressure is applied, only th middle of the horse is held or pushed, depending on the le you use.

Position No. 3—is the position for the halt when both leg are applied at once, equally strong. Individually applie they influence sharp turns where the hindquarters are pushe around into the desired direction. No. 3 is also the positio for the legs at the trot and faster gaits.

Position No. 4—one leg at a time (in combination with a opposite leg) will cause the horse to hold the hind quarters o push them around, as in acute turns where either the fro feet or hind feet, respectively, are used as a pivot.

Study these carefully and use these two pages to figure ou for yourself the results of various combinations of aids.

LEG AIDS IN ACTION

Knees remain firm to saddle. Lower leg opens away at right angles to horse and then back. Photo shows right leg open to limit, left leg in normal closed position. Outlines show each leg in opposite position. Notice heels are not brought in contact with horse. Leg aids may be applied equally or with different pressures, as they are moved into position.

Showing hand positions and the four leg positions, from above. Notice the left leg in No. 1 position and the right in No. 2. Reason is—Cadet started to move to left and leg was brought forward to hold him still.

White outlines show direction of hand movements from normal to limit of increased tension as in halting. Hands bend at wrist, lower fingers turned up to accent tension on snaffle reins.

From "Riding and Schooling Horses"
Lt. Col. Harry D. Chamberlin, New York, 1934

Quiet Hands

When confidence, relaxation and a fairly secure seat are established, the beginner should next bend all efforts toward keeping the hands quiet while maintaining a steady, light feel on the reins.

. . . until the seat is steady and the rider confident and relaxed, it is absolutely impossible to have "good hands." The old adage, "No seat— no hands," is indeed true. At this stage of instruction, however, quietness *of hands,* not finesse *in the use of them, is taught. The beginner should at first ride with loose, floating reins, and little by little he must learn to keep continuous, light and unvarying tension on the bit, with reins stretched softly taut. Of course, periods of rest with a loose rein are frequently given the horse. The rider should never support his weight or maintain his balance through leaning backward and pulling on the reins. (pages 49–50)*

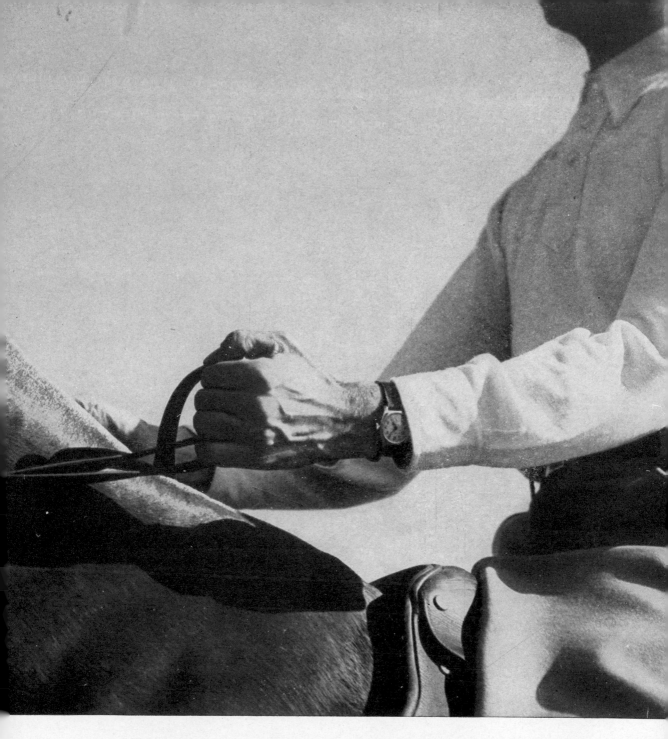

Showing lightness, yet sufficient strength of hands on reins.

Forearms parallel with horse.
Back of hands, wrists and forearms form a straight line.
Wrists soft, both vertically and horizontally.
Knuckles vertical.
Thumbs on top, lightly and firmly on bight.*
Lower fingers extended just enough, so that only slight flexing is sufficient
to increase contact (tension on reins) with horse's mouth.

See "Experimental Note" page 47.

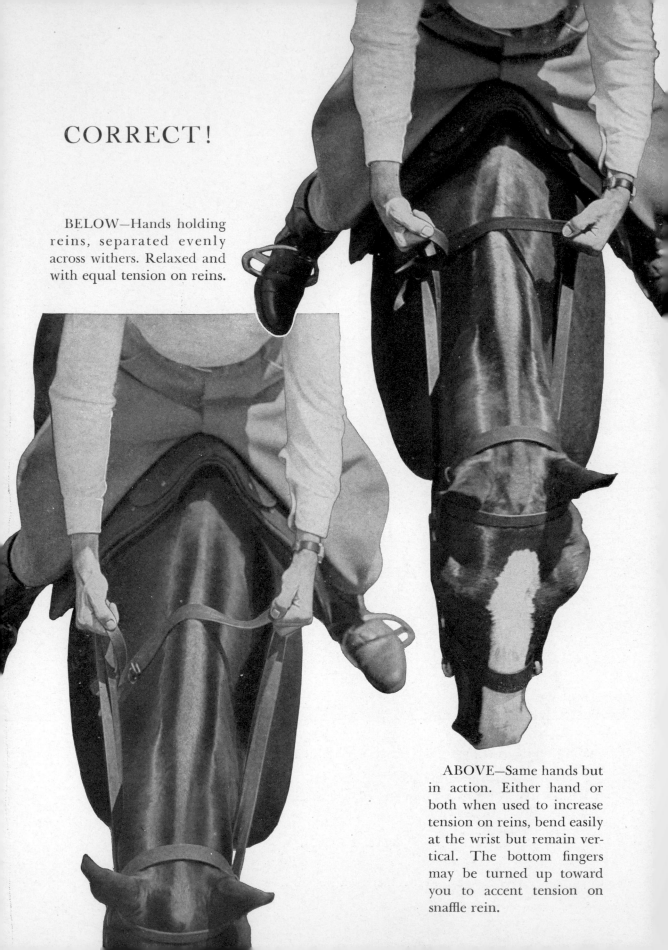

CORRECT!

BELOW—Hands holding reins, separated evenly across withers. Relaxed and with equal tension on reins.

ABOVE—Same hands but in action. Either hand or both when used to increase tension on reins, bend easily at the wrist but remain vertical. The bottom fingers may be turned up toward you to accent tension on snaffle rein.

INCORRECT!

This is *not* the way to use the hands on the reins because you cannot regulate the tension on the reins if your forearm and wrists are not free and flexible. You cannot have soft hands if their movements are restricted by the position shown.

Compare this picture with those on the opposite page. Study them and try the three positions yourself, over and over again. Try to use each hand in alternate positions. See for yourself how very important this part of the instruction is.

1. Hands show lower fingers relaxed. Tension on reins even and light. Legs against horse in No. 2 position, without pressure.

2. Left hand bends at wrist, as left leg is brough back into No. 3 leg position. Lower fingers of righ hand relax tension on reins.

These hand movements are exaggerated so that you may see the increas tension being exerted by the lower fingers on the snaffle reins.

3. Both legs are in normal position as right hand straightens horse's head and neck. Relax lower fingers of left hand.

4. Right hand increases tension as right leg is brought into No. 3 position, with pressure.

The hands and legs are working in unison. Lean forward and your weight ...d would be the final signal pushing the horse into movement from the spot.

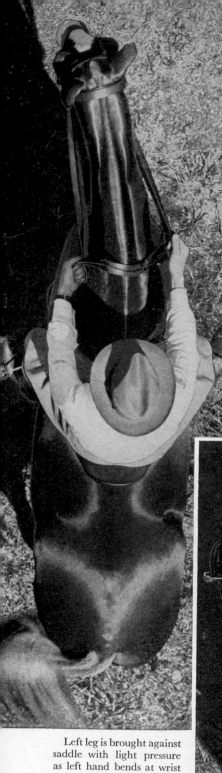

PRACTISE BENDING THE HORSE—FROM FRONT TO REAR, ON HIS MIDDLE. DO IT SLOWLY AND GENTLY WITHOUT SHIFTING WEIGHT IN SADDLE AND HORSE WON'T LEAVE THE SPOT

NOTE: The picture in the middle was taken from a more vertical position. In all three the position of the body was actually identical.

Left leg is brought against saddle with light pressure as left hand bends at wrist with lower fingers turned up. Right leg without pressure but in contact with saddle, as right hand remains passive but with lower fingers relaxed.

This bending to the right is exactly the opposite of the other, of course. Work it out for yourself. Remember—do not jerk reins, do not shift weight. Do it slowly.

PRACTISE TURNING AIDS WITH REINS
IN ONE HAND—IN PLACE

REMEMBER—
If you lean forward during these movements, the weight aid would signal the horse to move from the spot.

———

PASSIVE. Hand over withers, fingers relaxed, legs evenly weighted in 2nd position.

TURN TO LEFT— lower fingers increase tension on reins as hand twists up to you. Left leg with pressure at 3rd position.

TURN TO RIGHT— bend at wrist as upper fingers only increase tension on reins—right leg in 3rd position with pressure, as left goes to 2nd.

HALT—In slowly *repeated* movements (until horse halts) bring the hand toward you with even tension on all reins as legs, in 3rd position press firmly.

Practise these to see with how little effort you can complete the movements. Watch for evenness of rein lengths.

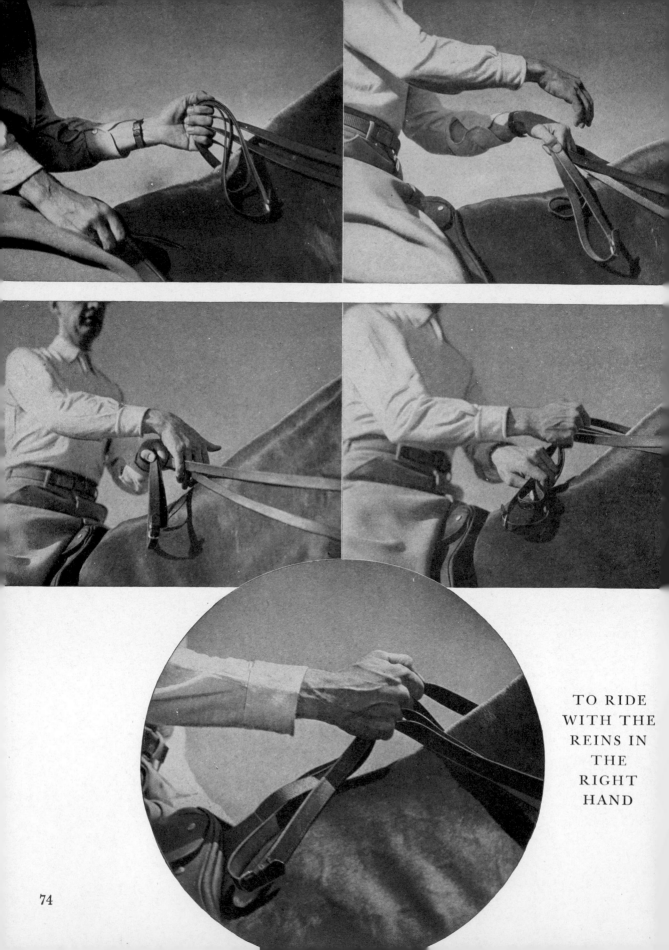

TO RIDE
WITH THE
REINS IN
THE
RIGHT
HAND

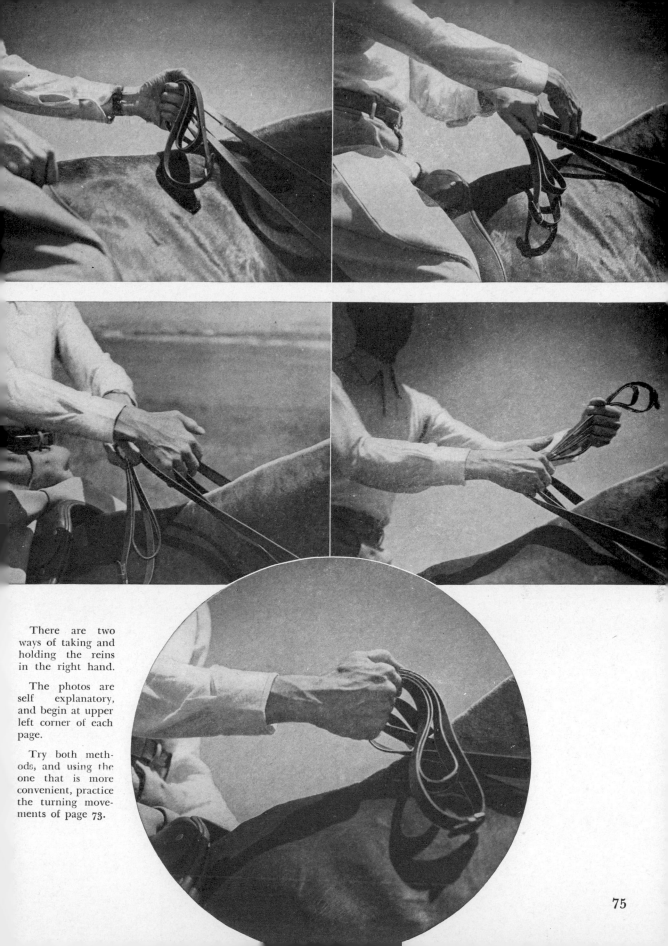

There are two ways of taking and holding the reins in the right hand.

The photos are self explanatory, and begin at upper left corner of each page.

Try both methods, and using the one that is more convenient, practice the turning movements of page 73.

To lengthen one rein. Relax fingers on reins and with free hand select and pull forward to desired length. Check the same rein on other side for evenness, of course.

ADJUSTING LENGTH OF REINS WHEN HELD IN ONE HAND

To shorten one rein. Relax fingers on reins and with free hand select and pull to rear through fingers holding reins. Check with the other side of same rein.

When reins are all too long, shorten with free hand by taking hold behind other hand which, relaxing fingers, slides down along reins to correct position.

TO ACQUIRE AND
MAINTAIN STEADINESS
OF SEAT WITH
THE HORSE IN MOTION

A TRAINING PERIOD

The first thing you must do is settle yourself deeply into the saddle and stay there comfortably, enjoying it. When this is accomplished, you will be in a position from which you may apply the aids properly and effectively.

You can accomplish this best by learning to ride without using the stirrups. This will help bring the inner uppermost thighs down close to the horse because the legs must hold more *by weight* alongside the horse rather than by gripping to him. The knee and hip joints must be relaxed—otherwise you make the mistake of gripping hard with the legs. This causes resistance and stiffness in the back—therefore, uncomfortable pounding.

One secret of riding is, of course, an ability to keep the body relaxed at all times. This means just two things—a limber or springy, though *erect*, back and a *supple* waist.

To acquire a limber back and waist put the horse into a walk with the aids specified. With your feet out of the stirrups, either hand holding the reins, you repeat the same series of limbering exercises shown you in acquiring the seat, on page 53.

Be careful to make your successive movements as smooth as possible.

As you gain confidence with experience, urge your horse into the slow trot. This is the gait just beyond the walk. You sit down as described above.

Knee and hip joints relaxed, back erect but springy. Shoulders square and head back. Legs down, ankles relaxed. Repeat again the above exercises, at will, as often as possible, but slowly always. This slow trotting properly done is the best possible means of acquiring a firm seat on a horse. At the same time it brings the confidence of the good rider.

If you are in doubt as to your ability to learn to sit out the slow trot, study carefully the pictures in this section. Then try again, in short periods, but take it easy, mentally and physically.

Let's learn to ride!

From knees down, open and close legs simultaneously on horse in softly repeated motions. Lean weight aid forward slightly as you do this, and relax the fingers so that he may go forward. As he starts off let your body come back (by extending the arms at elbows) to a comfortable erect position as you see. If he slows up use your legs and weight again. Walk him like this until you feel at home in the saddle and settling down. Keep your chest up, but not inflated.

Repeat the leg aids for the walk, but faster, weight aid further forward, until Cadet breaks into a slow trot. This is more a change of gait than increase of speed. Now, open your shoulders, head back, hands, arms and legs relaxed, everything "hanging." The legs feel a loose hold on the saddle which is fine, because you now feel your weight entirely on the inside uppermost part of your thighs and front area of your buttocks. On these fleshy regions you roll your weight, while your waist and hips act as a "universal joint" for the upper body.

THE SLOW TROT, WITH REINS IN ONE HAND

Cadet slow-trotting beautifully at a speed little beyond that of a good walk. Yet you see all his four feet clear of the ground. This is called the limit of suspension or upward thrust of the horse, in motion. But you, having been a good student are sitting down gracefully and therefore comfortably, because your weight is being rolled on the inside portion of the thighs and seat as described while your back remains limber, yet erect. This cushioned action protects you from the hard upward thrust caused when the horse's feet strike the ground. Any hard gripping to the saddle now will hinder the smooth operation of the "rolling" seat.

This is the same slow trot, but at almost the lowest point—as the horse's (diagonally opposite) feet strike the ground. Compare this picture and the one opposite. Isn't it graceful and easy? Learning to ride at this stage may be uncomfortable sometimes, until the legs "come down," but—the seat you acquire when successful will never leave you.

Try now, slowly, to do the same limbering exercises you learned before, but keep the horse moving regularly by using the leg aids. If it helps, leave off the spurs.

Slow trotting without stirrups is a dividend paying exercise. A good tip is to begin after about five minutes of checking the seat. After this take up the stirrups—and do you feel the difference?

From "Illustrated Horse Breaking"
Capt. M. H. Hayes, London, 1908

Pulling and Running Away

I can draw no line of distinction between these two vices, except one of degree; for animals which would be uncontrollable runaways with some men, would be only hard, or even moderate, pullers with other men. Besides, circumstances alter cases: for instance, I have ridden horses which it would be impossible for me to pull up in a race, chase, or sharp burst with the hounds; but which I could easily control when hacking, even in company, or on parade. I shall, therefore, for convenience sake, consider running away as an extreme form of pulling. Before beginning a discussion on this subject, I must candidly state my disbelief in any system of pure breaking by which a violent, masterful puller can be made permanently quiet for an indifferent rider to keep in control at fast paces under exciting circumstances. It is worthy of note that a fine horseman not alone holds an unruly animal in check; but also teaches him habits of discipline by the application of the "aids." (page 304)

WALK, HALT, SLOW TROT, TROT, CANTER AND EXTENDED GALLOP

At this point all the slow, rather boring study of the past begins to show results. Even the pictures get more interesting. Why shouldn't they? There are few things alive more interesting than the horse well ridden.

We spoke before of the "genius" of the good rider. We spent time analyzing that seemingly amazing ability to handle a horse simply and well.

We promised you that same genius and by the same means that all good riders acquired it. You should now be in a position from which you may judge for yourself both your own work and the merits of the school.

Riding a horse is a simple process and must remain so, because the horse is a simple minded animal. We repeat—for your everlasting remembrance—that what seems to be complicated mystery is nothing more than subtle though carefully applied signals given by the rider to the horse.

Have a nice ride!

Your appearance mounted, ready to ride. You and Cadet combine to make this beautiful picture because you are both alert and at ease with each other.

Notice the straight line from elbow to horse's mouth, hands light but firm, fingers relaxed. Legs close, without pressure, heels down. Check details with photos on pages 50–58.

84   Photo at right—how do you know the reins are too long? Is this stranger's seat correct? How about his feet? Compare with above. Which one seems balanced on the horse?

Weight aid forward, from the waist, hands releasing horse's head and shoulders, as your legs (from knees down) press and open, and repeat, until he steps out into a good live walk.

The white line represents your position as on the opposite page. Now, how far forward did you move your body, in inches? Try it again and again from the standstill and reduce your weight and leg aids, gradually, to a minimum of motion. It can be done easily. But, let the horse walk at least twenty feet between halts.

NOTE: *Before you actually try the walk, study the HALT on page 87.*

Photo to left. The entire movement overdone. Too much rider's legs and weight. Horse was not properly at attention to begin with. Horse's front legs therefore lazy.

The walk from above. Hands evenly balanced, in good contact with horse's mouth.

Turning at the walk. Lower fingers of right hand, closing, increase tension enough to turn horse to right as lower fingers of left hand relax on reins. Right leg in No. 3 position, light pressure only, because of gait. Why? Should the aid of body weight be employed in this movement?

Cadet is brought to a halt from the walk. Hands are closed at even tension, and bent (at the wrist) toward you as forearms show strength by being brought back slightly. Weight aid brought to rear position. White outline represents you at a standstill. Check with pages 64, 65. Practise the complete standstill, walk and halt process and see how little the aids may be used to get smooth results. Try for instance, not to move forearms to rear. It can be done.

Photo to right. Seat not down, shoulders and entire weight too far to rear. Criticize legs and reins and attitude of horse as they reflect on rider.

Slow trot, from above. Note lightness of hands as left hand flexes on reins to keep direction.

The slow trot. Compare with **Page 81.** Note that now, with a small part of the weight balanced on stirrups the weight aid is forward as it should be. Smoothness of "rolling seat" is still there because there is only a *light* pressure on stirrups. Strong pressure now would stiffen knees, hips and back. Legs in No. 2 position.

A beautiful gait.

Slow Trot!—slow trot!—it is the best possible means of acquiring and maintaining good seat, legs and suppleness on horseback! Practise it for at least five minutes of every half-hour of riding. Also, you must try to keep your hands from bobbing up and down—by flexing your wrists and elbows. Try it.

The normal trot. As you apply stronger leg aids, your weight is brought further forward at the waist to balance over knees and stirrups. Your back remains hollow as you rise a few inches forward and above the saddle, using the knees and lower legs as a base. You do not come down *hard* onto the saddle at the fall, but rather onto the forward part of the buttocks and inside corners of the upper thighs (the same regions used in slow trotting). Knees and calves press firmly to the horse as heels are pushed down hard. In the above picture you are posting on the left foot, which means that you come down as the horse's left front foot strikes the ground. As Cadet springs forward, over his left front foot, you will be lifted above the saddle. While the right front comes down and strikes—you maintain (or hold) your weight above the saddle, balanced on your inner thighs, knees and stirrups. You can tell the progression of the front feet by watching Cadet's shoulders. After trotting for several minutes on the left foot, sit down as the right strikes and continue posting,—but on the right foot this time. Remember, you will pull Cadet's mouth, if your hands rise and fall during the trot.

The trot, from above. Note that even at an increased gait the hands are still light on reins, and separated. You are still posting on the left foot.

The turn at the trot. Notice how nicely balanced the tensions are on the lower fingers of both hands. You see, it is *not* necessary to twist the body, swing arms, or pull the horse in turning. Your body is exactly in line with the angle of the horse at all turns. On which foot are you posting?

THE CANTER OR GALLOP

From the "Manual of Equitation," French Army, 1912
Translation by the U.S. Cavalry School

The importance of the gallop requires that the rider be familiar with all details of this gait, for the manner in which the horse takes it, keeps it, modifies it, or leaves it has great influence on its value. Furthermore, this one more or less complicated movement brings out all the rider's skill and requires implicit obedience on the part of the horse. In obtaining it the rider may apply all the principles set forth in training and he may demonstrate in detail the role and value of the aids . . .

The horse at liberty takes the gallop in different ways according to the circumstances which provoke it. That is, by a sort of loss of balance in throwing his weight forward, or by engaging his hocks under the mass in balancing himself.

When the rider desires to obtain the gallop by use of the aids he must consider the effects which the hands and legs may produce. . . . In order that the horse may understand that the sensation he receives calls for the gallop, he must first be placed in such a position that all confusion and hesitation are removed and only one movement is left to be executed—the one demanded. Position should always precede action, regardless of whether the horse takes the gallop through loss of balance or while in perfect balance.

. . . The gallop is characterized by one lateral pair of legs being more advanced than the other: thus in the right gallop (right lead, ed.) the two right legs are more advanced than the two left legs, and vice versa.

The canter, slow and easy. The weight aid brought sharply forward, as knees and calves close with the saddle in a "velvety" grip. The back is hollowed and kept that way by pressing buttocks to the rear, which also helps to force the heels way down. All this requires the inner parts of the thighs, knees and calves to be in close contact with the saddle, firm, but not rigid. Arms extended, giving with Cadet's neck and head as your legs hold strong in No. 3 position. The impulse of the horse at the canter is entirely from the rear. Study the detailed "Story of the Canter" which follows, and you will see why and how.

THE STORY OF THE CANTER
ON THE RIGHT FOOT, OR LEAD

Here you see Cadet at the last diagonal beat of the *trot*. You sit down as the left forefoot strikes the ground and your left hand increases tension on the reins as you remain seated, right leg firm as left leg, brought into No. 4 position, hastens use of horse's left hind leg.

THIS IS THE FIRST BEAT OF THE CANTER

Your left rein, with increased tension, carries Cadet's head to the left, restricting his left shoulder, as your right leg, in No. 1 position, holds his right shoulder to the front. The horse's left hind leg is then placed on the ground in support first—to maintain the balance of the hindquarters, as you see. This is called the first beat or tempo of the canter. Your seat in the saddle is down, weight aid forward.

Here is the FIRST BEAT of the canter as it appears from above. Left hand carrying head to left, right hand passive. Weight down. Notice your left leg applying pressure, but a bit too strong.

WHAT TO AVOID IN CANTERING

Seat excellent, but elbows locked to sides, hands weak, reins too long.

Reins too long, back hunched, seat insecure.

Back and seat excellent, but reins too long. Toes turned out at right angles force inside of knees away from saddle.

SECOND BEAT OF THE CANTER

Left front and right hind feet strike the ground as shoulders go down, hindquarters start up. You sit firm, as you were.

THIRD BEAT OF THE CANTER

Now follow him with even tension on both reins as he straightens out. His weight now on his right front as his hind feet leave the ground ready for the period of

SUSPENSION

All four feet off the ground. The left hind will strike the ground first, completing the cycle of left hind, right hind with left front, and then right front. These are the first, second and third beats of the canter, on the right foot or lead. The beats of the left lead are right hind, left hind with right front, and then left front—after which is the period of suspension.

This entire series shows the process of putting the horse into the right lead at the canter. That means that as he gallops, his right front foot will reach out to the front further than the left. In a riding ring, you go into the right lead when you are making the turns to the right. On the left lead when you turn to the left.

Study the canter process carefully. Then try it on both leads, but first—be sure your horse has been trained to both right and left. Walk your horse between periods of changed leads.

Canter, from above. Third beat. Left hand is still a bit strong on rein, as right leg in No. 1 position holds shoulder.

Turn at the canter—same third beat. Notice that the inclination of your body is again matched with the horse even at the increased speed. Notice how nicely your fingers are operating on reins. Left leg in No. 4 position to hold the hindquarters in the canter.

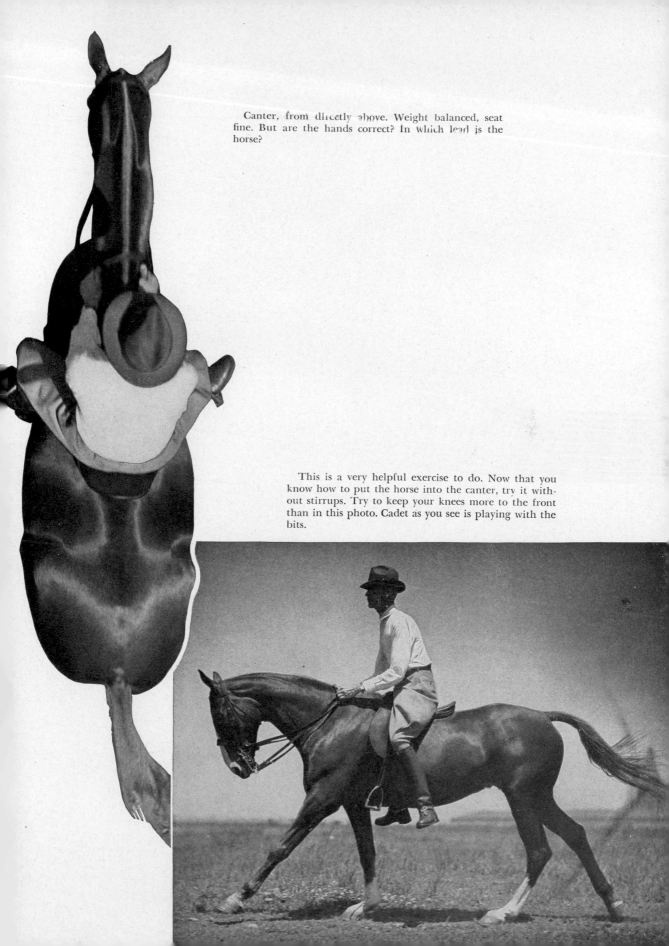

Canter, from directly above. Weight balanced, seat fine. But are the hands correct? In which lead is the horse?

This is a very helpful exercise to do. Now that you know how to put the horse into the canter, try it without stirrups. Try to keep your knees more to the front than in this photo. Cadet as you see is playing with the bits.

THE EXTENDED GALLOP

This gait is taken up from the canter

Your weight is brought more sharply forward, at the waist, as the hands take up the reins rather short, but without restraining the horse's head.

The leg aids are applied with greater strength at the calves to start, after which they rest close alongside the horse, ready to urge him forward if he slackens speed.

In perfect form, this picture is its own best description. Compare it with the canter. Then try it. Keep your back hollow—thighs, knees and heels down strong as the buttocks are raised slightly from the saddle and pushed to the rear. You will notice that your shoulders are being used very definitely now to maintain balance at this speed.

After a few minutes' run, slow him up *gradually* by a series of "half-halts" to a walk, and then halt. Now check your seat all over again. Then a short trot and off again into the canter and gallop.

Second beat of the gallop, right lead (same as on opposite page).

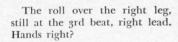

3rd beat, right lead, horse is about to roll over the right leg.

The roll over the right leg, still at the 3rd beat, right lead. Hands right?

Suspension—all four off the ground, notice the use of Cadet's right leg.

JUMPING

A THOROUGH PROCESS OF TRAINING THE RIDER
TO MAINTAIN HIS SEAT, BALANCE AND FORM
WHILE JUMPING THE HORSE. THE ONLY GOOD
JUMPING IS THAT WHERE BOTH HORSE AND
RIDER ENJOY IT. THIS MEANS THAT YOU MUST
CONVEY TO YOUR HORSE IMPLICIT FAITH IN HIS
ABILITY—BY CAREFUL RIDING ON YOUR PART!

"Jumping a horse," as it is known, is simple enough as an objective on the rider's part if the horse can jump. Cadet has been trained to jump up to two and a half feet, which is all the height necessary for basic instruction.

Height is not as important in jumping, at this stage, as is manner of going. As a matter of interest the crack military teams both here and abroad, train their horses today over jumps which are low but broad. Concentrated effort is put into teaching the horse to jump perfectly at a regular gait and without refusing. You will see them jump, without wings on either side of the obstacle almost invariably, which is further proof of the correctness of the system.

Now, how about you!

The first thing you do is to take a walk over to the jump when no one is using it and examine it. Forget the horse for the present. Your job now is to make yourself familiar with the ground around the jump and the various parts that make up the obstacle to be hurdled. The uprights at both ends are called posts. The long poles that lie horizontally from one post to the other are called bars. Of course you can adjust these bars to any desired height, but they must be arranged so that they will fall easily to the far side if tapped by the hoofs. "Wings" are the white side fences that you see at shows, forming an entrance chute to the jumps. They are unnecessary to good jumping and *you* will learn to jump by *riding* your horse at a regular gait, and in complete control all the time, right over any jump the horse can make.

To begin your training, lower two bars at the jump to rest parallel on the ground, from post to post. Two are better than one because it encourages extension of the horse's body for easy crossing.

Now (to give yourself the idea) being dismounted, from a distance of about fifteen feet, walk in a straight line, evenly between posts, across the two poles on the ground, and continue on the other side for about the same distance before turning around in a circle to return to where you started. This time try to regulate your strides so that you cross the poles without hesitation. You will notice that you have to extend your stride more than for normal walking, and that you must have a higher knee action. This same extension is what you must encourage in your horse when jumping. Now that you understand what the horse must do, even with bars on the ground, consider carefully the aids necessary to increase the normal to an extended walk, slow trot, trot and canter without breaking the gait.

It is not hard to acquire this knack of "rating" the horse to an obstacle and over. But only conscientious practice and study on your part will do it.

Next, take your horse. Check equipment. Mount slowly, deliberately. Flex your hands and arms, one at a time. Take reins in both hands. Check your seat several times. Ride your horse out at a regular walk first, and after a few minutes of this try to extend the walk by using the aids carefully. When you feel you have the horse moving properly head him straight toward the jump, so that he arrives there at a point about twenty feet from the middle, headed squarely between posts.

NOTE: Some horses jump better on one hand than another, so find out which one is preferred. Then make your circle in that direction.

Walk your horse, calmly, between posts, over the middle of the bars on the ground. Use walking aids with slight increase of strength. Continue to walk ahead for the same distance as the approach, before turning around. Repeat often.

Slow trot through. Use the aids to keep him going through between the posts at the middle, by increasing strength against the opposite side if he tries to move out of the straight line. Take it easy. You pay no attention to the bars! Don't let the "jump" change your well-earned form! Repeat often.

The *normal posting trot* through. Now, it is even more important to learn to control his stride so that his step over the bars will be in cadence with those approaching. Do this by using the hands *lightly* on reins to restrain or release him. Repeat.

Canter through. Do it slowly. Watch his stride now, more than ever. As a rule, by now, the horse will measure his stride to a jump naturally, if you have encouraged him by good hands and balanced seat. Repeat all over again.

Do these over and over again. *Don't* look down at the bars. Look ahead between the horse's ears.

These four pictures present an excellent opportunity to see how the weight aid moves forward, maintaining balance as speed increases.

107

At the Walk—Repeat often.

The whole process over again, of acquainting yourself with the basics of jumping, but this time without the use of the stirrups. The aids are the same as with stirrups, but greater dependency is placed on a supple body and the firmness of your seat.

At the Slow Trot—Your legs are turned out too much, even if they are being used strongly. Try again.

Normal Trot—Knees and lower legs are turned out too much, which is why your seat is a bit high. Try again.

Canter—Forearms should be extended a bit to release Cadet's head. Compare with page 107. Try again.

THE HORSE'S MOTIVE POWER IS ENTIRELY IN THE HINDQUARTERS AND COUNTERBALANCED BY HIS NECK AND HEAD, IN FRONT. WHEN THE BARS ARE RAISED ABOVE THE GROUND THE HORSE MUST BE ALLOWED EVEN FREER USE OF HIS HINDQUARTERS TO ENABLE HIM TO LIFT YOU AND HIMSELF OVER THE JUMP IN ONE FREE, GRACEFUL MOVEMENT.

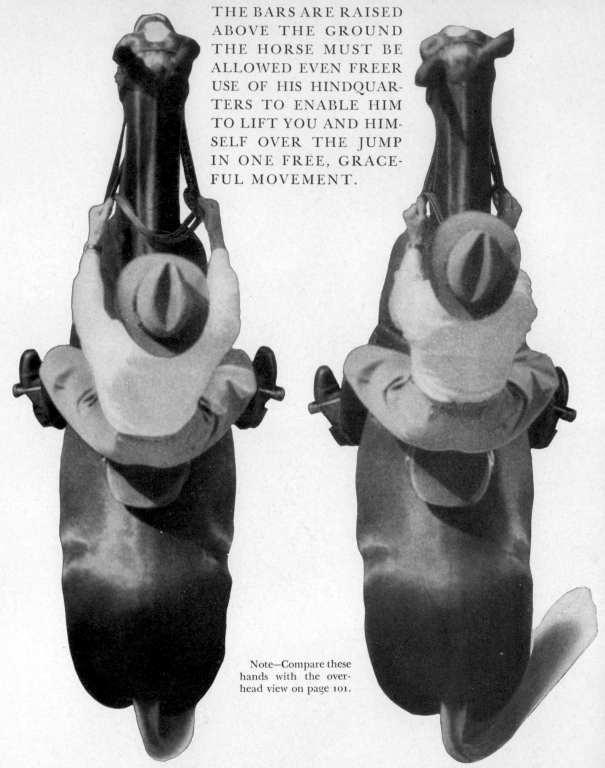

Note—Compare these hands with the overhead view on page 101.

Photo to the left shows the seat as used in the canter—from overhead. On the right, above, the seat as used for the extended gallop and jumping. Note the clearance of the saddle as the buttocks are raised when thighs, knees and stirrups take what little weight there was off the horse's back. The point of balance is brought more directly over the horse's shoulders. The horse now is encouraged to use his hindquarters more freely because, in this position you can extend your arms and permit him *freedom of head and neck* without giving up control. Compare this photo with page 102.

Give yourself some exercise cantering, very slowly. Drop stirrups. When you feel well down in the saddle and thoroughly at ease, slow up and repeat some of the exercises on page 53. Relaxed—walk your horse briskly, no stirrups, straight toward the jump. When twenty feet away take up the canter. Hands apart, the horse's head carried lightly between—your legs holding him firmly to the jump, take him over! Continue straight ahead for twenty feet while gradually reducing speed (within this distance) to a walk. Talk caressingly to Cadet. Rest, pat him on shoulders and neck. Walk him around quietly until you feel ready to try it again.

Repeat all the above, but use stirrups. This time, *as you begin to canter, assume the position for the extended gallop*—back hollow and buttocks raised. Do *not* increase speed. Try it and see.

A comprehensive view showing the horse and you balanced and jumping, completely at ease. Notice how well you use your thighs, knees and legs.

NOTES ON JUMPING

Don't use an extended gallop when approaching any jump in this course. A canter, well handled, is sufficient for most jumping.

The direct approach to these jumps should never exceed twenty feet—just enough to give you a good, live start in a direct line over the *middle* of the jump. Keep your legs ready for an encouraging push if he falters.

As you feel him extend his neck and head to get over, let your arms extend easily with him, but don't loosen your reins.

Once over, go straight on for another twenty feet before turning. Keep your heels down all the time, your head and chest up, shoulders relaxed.

———

". . . . the correct way to jump a horse is for the rider to lean forward, with his buttocks off the saddle while approaching the jump, during the jump, and until the horse takes a stride or two after landing . . . . with the balanced seat there is no good reason for doing otherwise. . . ."

LT. COL. J. K. BROWN.

Reins should be shorter (compare with lower photo)—hands away from horse, left foot turned in more like right.

Too bad that your left foot insists on turning out too much, and marring an otherwise perfect score.

Remember in all your jumping—use the seat of the extended gallop but at the slower speed of the canter.

113

A very good jump that would have been excellent if your forearms and wrists had not been so rigid. Try again—hands clear of horse, arms, elbows and wrists relaxed and flexible. See "Notes on Jumping," paragraph 3.

Good—in that the horse has his freedom and your legs are down. But watch the improvement if you succeed with above suggestions.

This is the fine result of training over a low but broad jump. Notice the extension and ease of the horse. He enjoys it immensely. You are doing very well yourself. Compare details with those criticised on opposite photo.

ANALYSIS OF THE SAME JUMP AS ON THE PRECEDING PAGE

Above photo is your "ideal" position (posed) with no movement.

Photo to the left shows what you did as you were in mid-air. The white outline indicates your position as it is in the "ideal." Try the jump again. Don't twist your head and shoulders. That is what caused your left foot to turn out. Watch the hands too.

Notice the extension of the horse as he exerts his power from the hindquarters.

RIDING IN THE ITALIAN STYLE SADDLE

POPULARLY KNOWN AS THE "FORWARD SEAT" SADDLE

Yoᴜ are finished with the basics of riding in an average type saddle. Now you are ready to try the Italian style jumping saddle shown on page 30.

This saddle is designed to be ridden with a short stirrup. By an expert it may be ridden with an extremely short stirrup—as practised by international jumpers and men of similar experience. But to complete a basic course such high ambition is not necessary. Remember, there is no hurry—even now. Therefore, take this saddle and check the length of stirrup (page 35). Now shorten the stirrup straps two holes. Mount exactly as you did before. You will notice that a shorter rein length is possible and this is what you need. You feel, because of your training up to now—a firm seat with a "tight-fit" feeling at the lower thighs and knees—but, on the whole, rather high in comparison with the seat you have been riding. You do like the forward thrust of this saddle, with its short stirrups, don't you? So alert!

The problem, then, is to get yourself down in *this* saddle, using the short stirrups, riding with the knees down and legs under; on exactly the same principles as in your previous saddle.

Go through all the limbering exercises you have done before for as long a period as 10 minutes at a time, but without using stirrups. At the end of each period place your feet in the stirrups and then check your seat. Trot your horse—slowly at first—until you rise to the trot with the same timing as in the training saddle. You may feel, as you try this, that you have a tendency to rise too high because of the short stirrups. But by closing your legs and pressing further down on your heels, "holding" above the saddle for a fractionally longer period, you can overcome that. Then try cantering—with your seat in the saddle. Now you will find that your legs fit even more snugly to the horse. Continue at very slow speed until you can ride with the now acutely bent ankle thoroughly relaxed.

All these requirements for the jumping saddle mean no more than this: you will maintain a balanced seat in this saddle in keeping with its designed purpose—balance with the horse at faster gaits and jumping.

Compare the position of your seat in the training saddle—as indicated in white outlines—with your seat in this saddle.

One—Your point of balance at the standstill is equal to that of the walk in the training saddle.

Two—Your hands are further forward but still in a straight line from the elbow to the horse's mouth.

Three—Your buttocks are in exactly the same place.

Four—Your stirrups are shorter and therefore your legs are still closer to the horse.

Five—Your knees are now a bit higher and further forward, but still down against the rolls.

But all the rules for maintaining the balanced seat as previously explained stand.

The normal trot (on the left foot) with the jumping saddle. The white outline represents your position at the same gait in the training saddle. The vertical line of balance is further forward now, but the design of the saddle permits your legs a firm base. You must be careful to maintain the same short diagonal rise at posting that you did in the training saddle. This means that your hip joints will have to hold you for a longer "rest" above the saddle until the left foot (in this case) strikes. All other rules for the trot hold.

First beat—

You put too much weight on your left hand.

Second beat—

Compare your wrist with those in other two photos. Which are correct and why?

Here you are riding out of the saddle at the canter, your weight in the legs and stirrups. In all three photos your buttocks should be extended more to the rear. This would give better balance control. As it is, your seat is too high, with your back not in very good control.

The white outline represents your cantering seat in the training saddle.

Cadet is on the right lead. The three photos (on both pages) show first, second and third beats of the canter. The next period is suspension—see page 103.

From "Riding and Schooling Horses"
Lt. Col. Harry D. Chamberlin, New York, 1934

How the Horse Jumps

. . . An animal with a short neck, such as a deer or dog, when jumping a high fence, pops almost straight up into the air, and lands on all fours simultaneously. A horse, on the contrary, by using his head and neck as a balancer, describes a graceful parabola, with his fore feet coming to ground well in advance of the hind. It is an interesting fact that the fore feet strike the ground and leave it again before the hind feet touch. *Inasmuch as this see-saw, or bascule, movement is accomplished as a result of the employment of the head and neck, the necessity for the rider's not interfering with their movements during a jump, is evident. All have seen a poor rider hanging onto the reins and pulling the horse's head high in the air, over the top of a jump. With his neck thus immobilized, the poor horse also lands on all fours simultaneously, and is said to jump like a deer. (pages 179–180)*

JUMPING IN THE "FORWARD SEAT" SADDLE

The problem of taking a horse over a jump remains unchanged when you change your saddle. You must still keep your hands evenly and lightly on the reins, although the reins may be shorter. Your seat must still be balanced with the speed of the moving horse, even though your stirrups may be a bit shorter. Your legs must still keep him moving at a regular gait. Your chest must still be up. Your back must still be hollow and strong.

But it will be easier for you to do all these things. The knee rolls and pads will provide a more secure place for your thighs and knees—so that you can travel more comfortably with the buttocks raised from the saddle as they (the buttocks) act as a balance weight or control. You must not treat the knee rolls as a bumper against which you stick your kneecaps. As on the training saddle it is only the inside surfaces of the lower thighs and knees that come close to the saddle. This recalls to you the requirements of the balanced seat for the training saddle. You will now keep your heels down further than you ever thought possible. They must never, particularly in this saddle, be allowed to rise.

The ideal form posed, for approach and up to the moment your horse leaves the ground. Although it can't be seen from here, your buttocks are raised and pushed to the rear. Study for details of head, hands, knees, etc. Try it.

Compare this with the opposite photo. What do you think of yourself?

Excellent in all respects. Seat out, weight in thighs, knees and stirrups. But try next time to use your right leg aid with lots of strength, plus increased tension on the left rein, to keep Cadet at the middle of the jump.

A good job, but compare with page 115.
Would you say that you did a better job with your back in one than in the other? Are you taking proper advantage of the saddle design? Is the horse doing as well?

Too much extension of arms. For a jump this size you are too strained and your back is weak. Reins flying, horse now out of control. Knees strong but lower legs are hooked into horse.

From "Principes de Dressage et d'Equitation"
James Fillis, Paris, 1890

The fundamental principle that stands out from the studies that I submit to the public, is that it is necessary to search for balance, lightness of the horse in forward movement, in impulsion, in order to obtain the most energetic results by the least effort.

Balance by the height of the neck flexed at the poll, not at the withers; impulsion by the hocks engaged under the center; lightness through the relaxation of the jaw; there you have my equitation in toto.

When we know that, we know everything and we know nothing. We know everything because we find these principles in all things. We know nothing because there still remains putting them into practice.

AND LAST—RIDING WITH THE HUNTING SNAFFLE

This combination of forward seat saddle and single snaffle bridle is an ideal outfit for riding. Why weren't you permitted to use it to begin with? Because this school wanted you to feel the confidence of complete horse control at the beginning. Now that your confidence is an established fact, it is time to learn to ride with a minimum of control rather than a maximum.

All the rules for the hand aids still apply. The braided effect on the reins gives you a better grip when the reins get wet; but learn to use the snaffle as lightly as you would a curb.

When you have made yourself familiar with this outfit, go through the entire course of instruction right from the beginning. By such attention to details are good riders made.

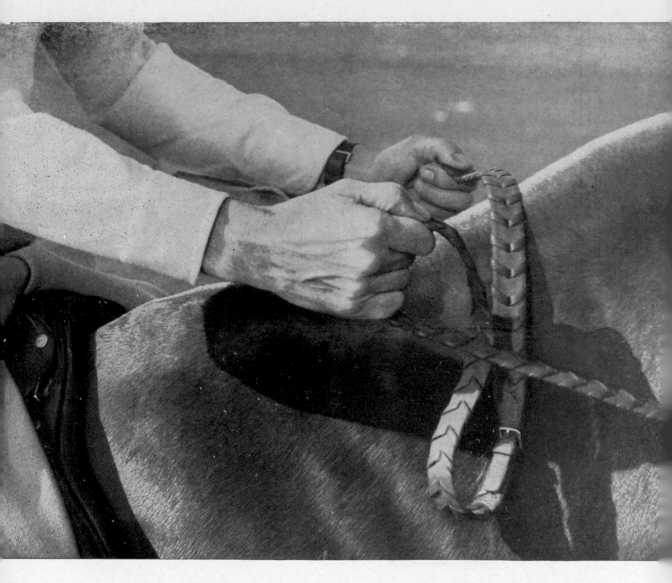

The attitude of the hands holding reins does not change with the bridle. Note the lightness, strength and flexibility in this picture. Compare it with others in the book.

Now look! If the back of your shirt is wrinkled evenly across it indicates a correct hollow back. How is the back in this picture in addition to several other faults? Compare with opposite photo.

135

TAKING SNAFFLE REINS
INTO THE LEFT HAND

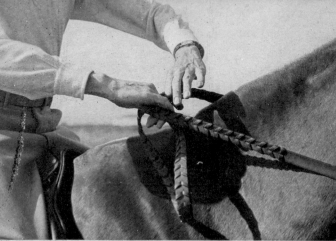

1. Turn hands together—and thumb and forefinger of right hand take left rein too. Left hand spreads and reaches over

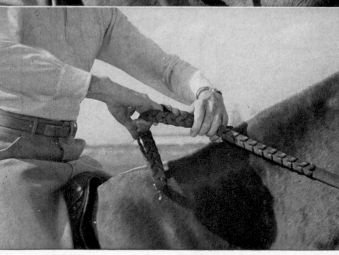

2. . . . to place *little finger between* both reins as next three come *over* both and close reins together, keeping thumb in back. Right hand maintains its hold on what is now the bight.

3. Right hand now takes bight and brings it over and in front of left hand which is now vertical again.

THE LEFT HAND HOLDING SNAFFLE REINS

"The attitude of the hands holding reins does not change with the bridle. Note the lightness, strength and flexibility in this picture." Compare it with others in the book.

Note: Turn to page 47 and compare the thumb position in both pictures. What has been your experience?

THINGS TO REMEMBER
WHEN LEARNING
TO RIDE

Take your time! Your horse is in no hurry. He is just naturally not the kind of artificially inspired animal you are. His life is not dedicated to finishing any job in a hurry. What may seem like hurry to you in a horse is usually fear on his part.

And so, our advice to you if you really want to enjoy riding a horse is to resign yourself to slowness, deliberateness and above all, calmness. Such qualities exhibited while learning to ride endear you to horses, even the most nervous of them. You will find out, and pretty soon too, that the only time you can really enjoy riding is when the horse enjoys your manners. That is the result of the author's personal experience and he has yet to hear a dissenting voice from more experienced riders.

If the horses you have ridden before do not act like Cadet, you are probably as much to blame as the horses. This course of basic instruction was designed to teach you how to ride an average horse and how to control him in a simple, effective system. *Study* what this book shows you—it's simple enough—and *practise* it.

Practise keeping your heels down!

If you hire your horses, search carefully for a stable that is clean and fresh smelling. You will soon find out that the horse reflects his stable and owner.

Keep your head and chest up!

There is no law that compels you to sit on your horse's back for an entire riding period. Dismount and take a walk with him—dismount and then rehearse the mounting process—and do anything else your common sense dictates or experience shows will make you thoroughly at ease with horses.

Practise keeping your ankles flexed!

When dismounting talk to the horse in a comforting tone and, once on the ground, go toward his head and pat him. Talk to him before you leave him if only for a moment.

Flex your shoulders, your arms, your wrists!

To lead your horse, take the position as in the first picture on page 34 and, closing your hand firmly on the snaffle reins, you turn his head in the direction you want to go. Then, without turning to look back at the horse, your hand firmly behind Cadet's chin, start to walk in that direction—slowly at first.

Keep your heels down!

HOW WE PREPARED
"RIDING"

Beginning sometime in early May of this year, we started on this job. The last picture was taken during the first week in July. About ten week ends covered the training and picture taking. Week ends is true. Every picture you see in this book and many others, with very few exceptions, were taken on a Saturday or Sunday, weather permitting. The entire preparation of negatives and prints was done during spare evenings as we found the time.

Our problem of course, was to get "the rider's viewpoint." How to do it? The saddle on the horse holding only one rider, we decided to get directly above the rider. To do this and still permit the rider room to jump when necessary, we needed a platform. It had to be a big one because we could not scare away Cadet. It had to be safe and steady enough so that we could keep Mr. Friduss and camera working safely on top. The top of the platform had to be twenty-seven feet from the ground, which distance gave us the area of sharp focus we needed. We finally found a concern that made what we needed and you see in these two photos what we used to get the results for which we strove—"the rider's viewpoint."